I0149097

EDUCATION FOR SPIRITUALLY CONSCIOUS LIVING

How Parents Can Give Children
The Education They Really Need
(And Why Schooling Can't)

ANDREW SEATON

Inspiring Stuff

Published by Inspiring Stuff
inspiringstuffpub@outlook.com

ISBN: 978-0-9806620-1-6 (pbk.)

A catalogue record for this book is available from the National Library of Australia

A political orator wittily compared our party promises to western roads, which opened stately enough, with planted trees on either side, to tempt the traveller, but soon became narrow and narrower, and ended in a squirrel-track, and ran up a tree. So does culture with us; it ends in headache... Do not craze yourself with thinking, but go about your business anywhere. Life is not intellectual or critical, but sturdy.

Ralph Waldo Emerson

*The more you know,
the less you understand...
Can you step back from your own mind
and thus understand all things?*

Lao Tzu

Cease trying to work everything out with your minds. It will get you nowhere. Live by intuition and inspiration and let your whole life be Revelation.

Eileen Caddy

CONTENTS

PREFACE

Thank you for opening this book. I hope that in it you might find inspiration and practical guidance for a more sane and rewarding kind of education for your children. (With apologies to teenagers, for simplicity's sake I will use the word 'children' to refer to young people up till adulthood.) I say "your children", because most often it will be parents and grandparents who have the motivation and opportunity to provide children with the kind of experiences I describe. Nevertheless, this book will be of interest to anyone with a serious interest in human nature and the philosophy and methodology of education.

I have extensive experience in education. I have been a teacher at both primary and secondary levels, an in-house then private consultant in effective learning and teaching and in school improvement, and an education academic specialising in 'new learning and new teaching' at an Australian university. In 2005, I completed a role-based PhD, with a thesis titled, "Investing in Intelligence: An Inquiry into Educational Paradigm Change".

In 2006, I finally concluded that there is no hope that institutionalised schooling can ever provide the kind of education that would support the full functioning of human beings. I resigned from my position in education academia to write and pursue other projects. Among these other projects has been the opportunity to begin to re-educate myself according to the insights gained in my doctoral research and my subsequent explorations.

In 2010, I self-published a book titled, *Deep Intelligence: Giving Our Young the Education They Really Need*. My notion of 'deep intelligence' is more or less synonymous with my understanding and experience of the notion of 'spiritually conscious living'—an awareness and way of being beyond the conceptual mind and the egoic sense of self, where one sees the true nature of reality and feels one's oneness with Being and connectedness with all that is. As we become more spiritually conscious in each moment, really present and awake, we see that much of what has kept us 'asleep' has been our habits of mind, what we thought we knew with our conceptual mind. We begin to experience that life is not intellectual, but at once more subtle, more real and more vital. We see that all things that truly matter—such as intuition, beauty, joyfulness, connectedness, creativity, spontaneity, inner peace—arise from beyond the mind, so long as the mind does not get in the way!

Our troubled world is mostly run by 'educated' people, in the conventional, institutional sense, whose minds *are* getting in the way!

But, in this book I outline how parents can educate their children in such a way that they are not bound by a conditioned mind. Such an education allows a person to live with deep intelligence, intimately and dynamically connected with life. An education for spiritually conscious living strengthens a child's ability to live with a flexibility, intuition and creativity that tap the spiritual depths of life.

This book is a substantial re-working of *Deep Intelligence*. In this book, I have shifted the emphasis to providing an outline of the practical things parents can do in support of the true education of their own children. I have also attempted to make this book more readable for people with no formal background in education.

I have removed two chapters about the futility of attempts at meaningful reform of the schooling system. Two other chapters have been repositioned. One of those chapters summarises the inadequacies and negative impacts of schooling. The other explains the complete inadequacy of the assumptions about human beings which underlie conventional schooling. I feel it is a more adequate discussion of educational theory, psychology and philosophy, from first principles. These two important chapters provide a strong justification for the approach to education outlined in this book. But I have positioned them after the more practical chapters, because some readers will feel they need no convincing on these topics, and others may find the reading in these sections more 'heady' and difficult than the chapters focused on activities, methods and conditions.

Readers wanting to move more deeply into their own spiritual awakening will find many of the activities described in this book as relevant and helpful for themselves as for their children. I also encourage these readers to read another of my books, *Spiritual Awakening Made Simple: How to See Through the Mist of the Mind to the Peace of the Here and Now* (see page 113.)

Andrew Seaton
October 25, 2025

CHAPTER 1

ENGAGING WITH WHAT IS REAL

What is the aim of education? Well, that depends on who you ask. This book is a brief guide for parents and grandparents about how they could educate their children. However, the *ways* in which it would make sense to educate a child are as different as the *aims* different people might have for education.

To begin with, then, I will briefly outline what I have come to understand about what well-functioning human beings can be like. (I will discuss this at much greater length in Chapter 6.) Some readers will see this description as a desirable aim for the education of their child. Others may not. For those who do, I will then go on to discuss the kinds of activities, experiences and relationships that are helpful (and some that are unhelpful) in nurturing this kind of functioning. This is important because, as the saying goes, "As the twig is bent, so grows the tree".

WHAT CAN A HUMAN BEING BE?

It is possible to educate a child in such a way that they keep, into adulthood, their sense of joy, enthusiasm and intense wakefulness. We can educate them so that they strengthen their ability to research, think, learn, adapt and do for themselves. We can educate them so that they are able to know people, objects, phenomena and situations freshly—not through rigid, conditioned patterns of memory, labels, definitions, expectations and judgements, but by a delicate yet profound relatedness or identity with them. We can educate them so that thoughts, people, things and events lose their power to trouble and manipulate them.

We can educate a child so that they keep and strengthen their sense of their own 'beingness', their formless, awareness self—a sense dependent on their ability to maintain awareness *beyond* thinking. We can educate a child so that their expression arises, not from a conditioned mind, but from their inner core, from a deeper aspect of

1

self than their intellect is able to fathom. We can educate them so that they live and act out of deep intelligence, as an expression of the formless intelligence within all life, rather than out of an illusory sense of self-as-separate.

In Chapter 5, I will discuss in some depth the negative impacts of schooling and why schools could never provide an education for spiritually conscious living. For the moment, I will make only some brief comments about why schooling is not able to nurture the type of functioning I have just outlined. The people running schools try, of course, to do a good job of educating children. However, schools operate on quite different assumptions about human nature and functioning and with quite different aims and methods. Let us look briefly at the idea of 'knowledge', for example.

SCHOOL KNOWLEDGE

Schools operate on the completely inadequate assumption that knowledge is a copy of reality. The thinking goes something like this. "The public sharing of concepts about the world makes them 'true'. We should collect all the most important and 'true' conceptual knowledge. Teachers can learn it in specialised subject areas. Then those teachers can pass enough abstract knowledge on to each child so they will be able to live a successful life in the future. Children can learn about the world by hearing about it from teachers, by reading about it, and by discussing, thinking and writing about it. Knowledge can be made a substitute for reality, a substitute for direct experience in the world and for acting in and on the world."[1]

However, as I will explain in greater depth in Chapter 6, knowledge is not really like this at all! Knowledge is *not* a copy of reality. It is merely an abstract *interpretation* of some aspect of the world that is constructed in an individual's mind. It is undoubtedly helpful at times, in limited contexts and practical matters, to label, define, categorise, analyse, evaluate and apply logic to elements of our experience. But we do not know something just because we have named and defined it.

Schools require children to engage day after day, year after year with this abstract kind of 'knowledge', torn out of context. The dominance of intellectual and linguistic processes in schooling reduces the dynamic aliveness of the world to crude abstractions. Combined with the constant pressure of assessment and grading, the forms of daily experience in schooling inhibit children's perception, behaviour and ability to attend to internal sensations, emotions, intuitions, insights and promptings. They disconnect children from objects, the natural world, other people and their own essence of Being.

EDUCATION FOR SPIRITUALLY CONSCIOUS LIVING

In contrast, education for spiritually conscious living supports each child in honouring, not just the authority of their own minds, but more profoundly, the authority of Being, the authority of the deeper Self that exists as who each child truly is. It is deeply emancipatory. It does not seek to strengthen or empower the sense of self-as-separate. But nor is it about children doing what society demands of them, and taking on identities society creates for them. Yes, the child is encouraged and inspired to have some engagement with practices and perspectives valued by the community within which they live. However, education for spiritually conscious living is not about adding to or shaping who each child is.

Unlike the technology that is schooling, education for spiritually conscious living is not primarily about preparation for an anticipated future. Rather, its main purpose is to make possible a certain quality of experience in the present. It is not primarily a means to an end. When we are preoccupied with outcomes, we cannot give total attention to the present. We block the guidance and creative power of Being. The greatest value of all activities in education for spiritually conscious living is not their outcome, but the peace-filled awareness of unlimited connectedness, the flow of Being that a child experiences due to being fully present.

Educational quality and value truly consist in the forms of relationship, experience and activity which contribute to growth in deep intelligence, growth in a child's ability to live intimately and dynamically connected with life. An education for spiritually conscious living does not focus on mastery of abstract bodies of 'human knowledge'. The end and means of education for spiritually conscious living is not learning, as such, but fully conscious living. It is cultivation of presence, of intuition, and of creative and purposeful doing. An education for spiritually conscious living awakens the faculties of consciousness and general abilities, such as self-management, various literacies, creative activity, participation in community and stewardship of the things and spaces in an individual's life.

Education for spiritually conscious living helps each child to be aware of, to understand, and to manage how they function. It shows them how habitual patterns of thought, emotion and behaviour may control and distort their perception. It shows them how they can experience the stillness of Being, their true self, and how they can

3

consciously manage their own creative energies. It recognises the need for respecting relevance and purposefulness from the child's perspective, and the value of significant levels of personal direction of action and learning. Such an education involves engagement with practices, procedures, texts and projects that foster fresh perception and experience of the stillness of presence, and that enhance the child's ability to function intuitively, to think practically, and to act creatively in relation to their felt interests and purposes.

Education for spiritually conscious living is a living thing, a living power, not an inert technology for creating a pre-determined product or outcome. A set of suggestions and guidelines can be given, but no set method or curriculum machinery to be adhered to rigidly. A 'program' of education for spiritually conscious living will provide young people with opportunities for involvement in a wide variety of real-world projects, focused activities and unstructured experiences.

The generic elements of an education for spiritually conscious living are also the generic elements of a dynamic life. They are the various faculties and processes of consciousness, including procedures for making, testing, expressing and applying meaning that are associated with various disciplines, such as the arts, the sciences, critical thinking and a variety of literacies. They are 'generic' in the sense that they are independent of particular bodies of knowledge.

An education for spiritually conscious living provides young people with encouragement and opportunities to experience the inner stillness of Being, a deep sense of self-as-connected-with-all-life. It provides encouragement to constantly bring their attention fully to bear on their present experience, so that their perception and experience of the world are not limited or distorted by habitual patterns of thought, emotion and behaviour. It gives the child a variety of kinds of opportunities for becoming conscious of, and for expressing, changing and transcending, their conditioned operating patterns—their thoughts, their body, their emotions, pains and fears, their perceptions and their relationships.

Education for spiritually conscious living provides a child with encouragement and opportunities to recognise intuitions, flashes of inspiration, and inner knowings and promptings that arise from the depths of Being, the formless organising principle within themselves and all life. It gives them inspiration and opportunities to give their actions and experience their full attention, so that they cultivate their ability to deliberately manage the creative power of consciousness with enjoyment or enthusiasm. It gives them inspiration, opportunities and tools to contribute their loves, inspirations, talents and abilities to the world.

KNOWLEDGE IN CONTEXT

So where does 'knowledge' fit, in an education that nurtures the fuller kind of functioning I have described? The knowledge or understanding an individual has of anything, is only one inseparable facet of experience. It cannot be meaningfully separated from the context of experience or from the individual's aims. In fact, every experience that involves some 'knowledge', also involves not only an individual's aims, but also selective and interpretive perception, emotion, judgement, action, memory and biochemical processes and energy flows throughout their body.

To grow into an adult such as I have described, a child needs lots of opportunities to engage in self-selected activities in real-world contexts. With lots of such rich and authentic experience, a child is much better prepared to live intimately and dynamically connected with life.

REAL-WORLD PROJECTS

You may be sending your child to school, or you may be home-schooling your child. Either way, there are many things you can do as a parent to educate your child for spiritually conscious living. One of those things is to encourage and guide your child in investigating and acting in and on the world around them.

Encourage your child to reflect on their talents, on the things they love to do with their talents, and on the ways they can give to the world of their energy, creativity and caring. I commend to the reader the book, *Nurture by Nature: Understand Your Child's Personality Type—And Become a Better Parent*, by Tieger and Barron-Tieger. It discusses the functional tendencies and preferences of the 16 Myers-Briggs personality types, in terms of the relative strength of intuition, feeling, thinking and sensing, and whether each of these functions is more extraverted or introverted in its orientation. Each of the 16 types is fundamentally different in terms of what energises and what drains them, how they look at the world and take in information, the criteria they consider when making choices and decisions, and the ways they respond to and organise the world around them. Four of the 16 types have a basically traditionalist temperament, four are experiencers, four have an idealist nature, and four are conceptualisers.[2] Given that people have these very different natures, an understanding of your child's psychological type, and your own,[3] will assist you greatly in sensitively guiding and supporting their education for spiritually conscious living.

Encourage your child to nurture and pursue those talents, interests and inclinations that come with a feeling of peace, enjoyment or enthusiasm, rather than of agitation and strong attachment. Support them in choosing, defining and exploring a real-world purpose, and in developing, evaluating, explaining, and where possible and appropriate pursuing, a course of action in relation to that purpose. Before taking up their project each new day, encourage your child to clarify their intentions, consider their likely consequences, and let go of anticipated outcomes. Then they can go about their activities with full attention and presence.

Your child may have a deep interest in a particular kind of animal, for example. It might be feasible to allow them to keep, breed and train some of those animals. They might do it on a personal scale, or even eventually on a commercial scale, right through to marketing the animals. In the process, your child will certainly learn a great deal about the many things involved. More importantly, though, they will be able to live out their inner creativity, enjoyment and enthusiasm.

Real-world projects may also be proposed by a parent, who inspires a child to undertake a project. You may nudge, guide and *inspire* your child to engage in a wide variety of pursuits, over time. These might include projects in 'their personal world', 'our natural world', 'our social world' and 'our technological world'. Whether they arise spontaneously, or through the inspiration of a parent, it is important that these projects are not self-indulgent or insipidly politically correct. They must have grit. They must confront realities, and most importantly, confront the necessity of obedience to the deepest reality, the deepest promptings within the child.

Many parents are engaged in home-schooling their child. Such parents may need help with engaging their child in real-world investigations in such a way that, in the process, they are able to satisfy some of the requirements of a government education authority. Having a more intellectual and research character than the more practical real-world projects I'm advocating as part of education for spiritually conscious living, real-world investigations can be used as devices for curriculum integration. For home-schoolers, they can enable mandated learning to be done in a context that is more meaningful to the child. To this end, I have provided in Appendix B an example of an outline and planning proforma for real-world investigations. I have also provided a list of real-world investigation topics that could easily be adapted to meet mandated curriculum requirements. These are intended to be suggestive only. They are merely provided as resources that could be used in constrained circumstances, in the spirit of leaning towards education for spiritually conscious living. Investigations such as I have outlined in Appendix B are intellectual in their flavour and mostly unrelated to a child's own life. As such, unless the child has a genuine personal interest, they don't really have a place in education for spiritually conscious living if there are no externally imposed requirements to engage with school-like knowledge.

The real-world projects that *can* really be an effective component of an education for spiritually conscious living, are ones that have a more personal and practical purpose and where your child's involvement is genuinely voluntary. They must have a genuine sense of interest and ownership, and their involvement must not be coerced. Even when inspired by a parent, these projects are undertaken in such a way as to lend themselves to as much self-management by each child as they are capable of, with parent support, rather than high levels of parent-directedness and control. Some years ago, I read a good summary of a principle of progression that parents can sensitively apply when helping a child to engage with and master any new activity or part of an activity. "I'll do it, you watch. I'll do it, you help. You do it, I'll help. You do it, I'll watch."

In guiding a child in their undertaking of a real-world project, it is important that you give careful consideration to the child's interests, needs, circumstances and functional tendencies and preferences (personality type). Consider, according to the nature of the project, the possible need for activities relating to orientation and clarification of the intention, to observation of conditions, to information-gathering, and to examination of beliefs and emotions previously associated with the situation.

SEEING THINGS FRESHLY
Also be mindful of assisting your child in putting aside assumptions, and in viewing the situation, or elements of it, passively and receptively. This allows creative and intuitive processes to come into play that may reveal deeper insights and new connections that move the child beyond existing patterns of perception, thought, emotion and action. Activities may then move to the drawing of conclusions in relation to the project's aims, to identification and location of resources, to application and engagement in the undertaking, and to monitoring, evaluation and reflection. These activities can be drawn upon in a very

flexible and dynamic way that is responsive to the unfolding of the project and to the child's engagement and responses.

An important role of the parent is to sensitively support the child in changing and letting go of beliefs, emotions and attitudes that have become habitual. Young people (any people) consider alternatives to a view they hold, *only when they are convinced of the inadequacy of their existing view*. They only let go of old patterns if (1) they understand why new experiential or logical evidence represents a contradiction of some aspect of their existing viewpoint and behaviours, and (2) *it is important to them* to resolve the contradiction. Real-world projects lend themselves to such liberating changes, because they are generally of enough interest to the child that it will be important to them to let go of inadequate or inconsistent beliefs and behaviours.

Parents can help a child to see that they are not a fixed set of beliefs, but can be in charge of their own mind and life. Show them *how* they can see, know and respond more freshly and authentically when their habitual ways prove inadequate. There are several explicit ways parents can do this. For example, you can sensitively ask questions to elicit your child's conceptions *and misconceptions*. You can encourage your child to elaborate on *their misconceptions* and delve into *the thinking, memories and/or emotions behind them* ("How did you arrive at *that* conclusion?"), rather than being pre-occupied, as school teachers typically are, with eliciting from children, or giving them, the 'right' answer or method.

Show your child how to support or critique their own and others' points of view on the basis of experiential and/or logical evidence. In *Spiritual Awakening Made Simple*, I discuss at length a simple process of questioning conditioned assumptions about the world, one's experience, or oneself, especially judgements about whether those things are good or bad. When we do this, we find that we cannot ever know for certain that our thought is true. And when we see through what the conditioned mind-body thinks things mean, in particular its judgements of good and bad, we are left with presence—awake to our true nature as peace and oneness with the spiritual essence of all life. This will be a most valuable process to assist your child with, and I encourage the reader to refer to *Spiritual Awakening Made Simple* for details.[4]

Parents can also sensitively guide a child to activities, experiments and texts to *create conceptual conflict*, such as, for example, experiments whose results are likely to differ from the child's assumptions or predictions. And a parent can suggest that the child step back from thinking, and just give sensitive attention to the object, creature, phenomenon, or whatever it may be, passively, receptively, non-analytically. The child can try to release themselves from what they *think they know* about it, and open themselves to a feeling of its patterns.

THE POINT OF IT ALL... BEING FULLY PRESENT IN THE NOW

Encourage your child not to be preoccupied with what they might see as the eventual outcome of a project.

One fellow I knew helped a group of 9-year-olds investigate a concern they had that there were not enough recreational facilities for children in their area. My friend encouraged the children to look into the matter and what could be done about it. The children conducted an audit of all the existing recreational facilities. They constructed surveys and gathered the opinions of other children and community members about whether they felt there were already enough facilities, and if not, what they thought was most needed. The children concluded from their research that there was a great need for an adventure playground.

They set about investigating where such a playground could be suitably located. They then turned their attention to designing what they thought would be a good adventure playground, taking into account child appeal, but also safety, durability, cost and related considerations. Inspired by their mentor, they then formulated a proposal for the local government. It included evidence from their research of the need for an adventure playground, their illustrated design ideas with rationale and approximate costings, and suggestions for possible locations.

The children did not really expect to hear anything more about it. However, some weeks later they received a letter from the local government. It said that they were impressed with the research, rationale and ideas for an adventure playground, and had passed the proposal to their planning department to consider its feasibility. I do not know the eventual outcome of this project. I have related this story in a couple of workshops where the question has been asked: "Wouldn't it have been a waste of time, and wouldn't it be a devastating disappointment for the children, if the local government didn't ever build the adventure playground?" I do not believe so, at all.

The allowing of what is, is an important aspect of spiritually conscious living. Be sensitive in any situations of your child having a disappointing, painful or unexpected experience or outcome, and explore the situation with your child non-judgementally. Explore questions about contexts, priorities, budgetary constraints and the different points of view people often have about particular things in life. It would be a great shame if you were to confirm or convey to your child a sense that any real-world project had been a 'failure' or a waste of time. Rather, in the context of this kind of education, support such activities *because it is living*, without the primary concern being attachment to a particular outcome. Encourage your child to let go of judgement, and be peacefully present with what is.

ASSESSMENT, FEEDBACK AND REFLECTION

In education for spiritually conscious living, there will be legitimate occasions for appropriate forms of assessment. For example, you may need to know, on occasion, the capabilities of your child, so you can give appropriate guidance and recommendations for suitable activities or more effective performance. And it will often be helpful to a child to give them sensitive but honest feedback regarding the activities and procedures they are engaging with. But the kind of education we are talking about here has no place for grades. It does not involve assessment for labelling or ranking children. Rather, let the feedback you provide for your child be descriptive and constructive.

It will also be helpful to your child to encourage them to reflect on the effectiveness of their own activities, expression and creations, when appropriate. What difficulties did they have, if any? How did they overcome them, or attempt to? What new discoveries did they make about how to use various forms of speech or writing, or perform particular tasks? How might they do these things more effectively next time? In what ways have their thoughts and feelings about the matter at hand changed?

Many valuable skills can be developed in the context of real-world projects, including various literacy skills. In the next chapter, we will consider some of the ways this can be done.

Notes

[1] See, for example, Hirst 1972, pp. 123-124.

[2] Tieger and Barron-Tieger 1997, pp. 15-38. The Myers-Briggs description of 16 personality types is based on the work of depth psychologist Carl Jung and the mother-daughter team of Katherine Briggs and Isabel Briggs Myers.

[3] There are websites where you can do a short, free test to discover your Myers-Briggs personality type. At the time of writing, one such is at 16personalities.com

[4] Seaton 2020, Chaps. 4-5.

CHAPTER 2

SUPPORTING THE DEVELOPMENT
OF LITERACIES

THE NEED FOR RELEVANCE
Many valuable skills can be developed in the context of real-world projects, including a variety of literacy and numeracy skills. Children learn for themselves at an early age the complex structure of spoken language. Have you ever wondered, then, why so many children still struggle with written language after ten or more years of schooling? The answer has to do with the relevance to their own lives that children see, or don't see, in literacy.

Children become proficient language users through a rich exposure to interesting and purposeful language use. They master it, when they want to. Just as with oral language learning, we do not need to obsess over explicitly teaching children the core structure of written language. Nor do we need to be preoccupied with trying to improve a child's language use. This only tends to produce feelings of inferiority in the child, to create a self-concept of 'incompetent language user', and to inhibit their use of language.

THE VALUE OF PURPOSE, FEELING AND FUN
Unless there is some specific disability, children will readily internalise language in the context of interesting and purposeful activities, and an emotionally rewarding atmosphere. Other forms of literacy, such as numeracy, visual literacy and computer literacy, are acquired and developed in similar ways. For young children, the purposefulness may simply be the fun they have in the interaction. A child's consciousness is more strongly characterised and influenced by feelings than by rational and analytical processes. The various forms of literacy are, fundamentally, communication—expressing and interpreting meaning. They are developed most effectively, not in formal contexts of mass instruction, but in interactions experienced in authentic contexts and as parent/mentor and child resonate with each other. Such relationship

quality is crucial to an education for spiritually conscious living.

When working with language-based texts (such as a book, magazine, newspaper, website and the like), a child needs to know the symbol system of written language. They need to become able to read or interpret text, and to use the symbol system to write or construct text. They must be familiar with the letters of the alphabet, and aware of letter-sound relationships (phonics) and how letters/sounds combine to form words. Such awareness contributes to the ability to recognise words, to build vocabulary and to spell. An awareness of the conventions of sentence and paragraph structure and text layout also strengthens the child's ability to read and write written text. However, it is important that parents do not allow analysis of language symbols and structures to dominate the child's orientation to language. Don't let it inhibit their spontaneous and intuitive acquisition, understanding and use of language.

When your very young child expresses themselves orally about an observation, need or personal interest or experience, you can occasionally write the spoken words. You can then read them aloud, followed by the child. The child can then be encouraged to write the words as phrases, sentences and paragraphs. In this way, the child begins to see written language as a useful *extension of their own power of speech*. However, it is important not to make the activity serious, or to over-verbalise or over-analyse language and other symbol systems.

Language learning will also be facilitated if you read to your young child most days. Text selection is important. Choose stories and non-fiction texts that your child finds fun or engaging. They should be texts that are related to your child's interests and talents, and ones that are uplifting and inspiring, that stir the young soul.

It is helpful, when reading to your child, to 'think aloud' occasionally to identify elements of the language code. This also helps you to model for your child specific strategies for making meaning from the text. For example, you might stop and 'think aloud' about an unusual letter-sound relationship you come across in a text. "Ah, I see! The 'fff' sound that is usually made by the letter 'f', like in the word 'funny', can also be made by the letters 'ph', like in this word 'phone'." You might occasionally 'sound out', syllable by syllable, a word that is long or unfamiliar (even if only unfamiliar to the child). You might 'think aloud' about the context of an unfamiliar word to clarify its meaning. Or you might occasionally re-read a sentence, to gain further clarity on its meaning.

Children can also be given lots of opportunities to have fun with sounds and words in games, and in hearing and creating rhymes, limericks and riddles. Here's one example of a game that connects decoding with making meaning. Take a sentence spoken by your child, and write it in large letters on some thin cardboard. Say, for example, "The rider fell off when the horse jumped over the log". Then cut each word out. Arrange the order of the words to show the original sentence. Read it aloud and ask your child, "Does this make sense?" Then re-arrange the words. For example, "the-log-fell-the-off-jumped-the-over-when-rider-horse". Read it out loud, pointing to the words as you go, then ask your child if it makes sense? Why not? (Don't look for a technical reason!) Make several other re-arrangements, with possibly some others that do make sense. For example, "the-horse-fell-over-when-the-rider-jumped-off-the-log". "Does this make sense?" "Yes!" Lots of laughter and useful language learning will result from this language game.

DEVELOPING SKILLS THROUGH USE IN AUTHENTIC CONTEXTS

Many of these activities with various forms of literacy can be contextualised within a child's real-world projects. Such projects can provide a wonderful context for developing literacy skills, because they help a child to see the skills as relevant to their own lives. As the child undertakes their projects, they will find the need to engage with a wide variety of texts or procedures. We can think of these as 'genres'.

A genre, as I use the term here, is any purposeful activity, spoken, written or acted out, which is typically done in a particular way, or in a particular sequence. For example, conducting an experiment, sending an email, making a telephone inquiry, buying something in a shop, and even playing a game of tennis, are each distinctive genres. An understanding of genres helps us to recognise and use language and procedures appropriate to particular situations. It helps us to participate effectively in the social and material world.

As your child finds the need to engage with a particular genre, you can model its construction and 'deconstruction', to ensure that the child becomes familiar with ways in which that genre may be used. When appropriate, you might draw comparisons with experiences the child may have had previously with similar genres. It can be very helpful (to both child and parent) to have some genre guides which include a statement of the purpose of the genre, a simple outline of its typical structure, a brief description of its characteristic language features and conventions, and a short example.

EXPLAINING TEXTS AND PROCEDURES (GENRES)

To illustrate what I mean, let's look at (or 'deconstruct') a letter of thanks. The purpose of a letter of thanks could be described as follows. An expression of appreciation may take a spoken form (for example, a 'vote of thanks') or written form (in a letter or email). Its purpose is to express thanks to one or more people, or to an organisation, for some valued contribution, assistance or consideration. The description I will give here is of a written letter of thanks such as might be sent to a person not well known personally, rather than to a familiar friend or relative.

The basic structure of a letter of thanks consists of four parts:

1. Initial details, including sender's address, date, recipient's name and address, and greeting.
2. The actual comments of appreciation are expressed, including a statement regarding the nature, time and place of the event or situation which formed the context for the help provided. Some indication might be given of how you or others benefited from the help provided. Also, recognition should be given of the efforts, time, expense or inconvenience experienced by the person, as appropriate.
3. A brief statement of well-wishing, or possibly of further association or involvement with them in the future, is generally made in conclusion.
4. Formal or semi-formal sign-off, including identification of the group or organisation you represent, if appropriate.

What particular language features and conventions characterise a letter of thanks? Well, it takes a polite, semi-formal tone. It is written in a mixture of present and past tenses. It makes use of full sentences and paragraphs. Paragraphs in typed letters are typically separated by a blank line. In hand-written letters the start of the first line of each new paragraph is usually indented. Linking words and phrases to do with description, benefits and thanks are used, such as "it was good to", "we learned a lot", "we appreciated", "thanks again". Common formal sign-offs include "regards" and "yours sincerely". In the case of a letter of thanks, the tone would usually be a bit less formal, so "regards" or the warmer "kind regards" would be appropriate sign-offs.

You can find a simple example of a letter of thanks in Appendix A, along with some other genre guides for your use. According to your child's need and readiness, provide a genre guide and spend some time discussing and modelling the genre and the processes and thinking that go into its construction. On occasion, you might even work with your child to create a genre guide.

The literacies and procedures outlined above and in Appendix A really constitute generic elements of a dynamic life. They have nothing to do with the mastery of abstract bodies of school knowledge. The end and means of such activities is not learning, as such, but the cultivation of purposeful and effective doing, adaptation and interaction in the social and material world. Such activities enhance children's ability to function intuitively, to think practically and to act creatively in relation to their felt interests and purposes.

I have explained above that mastery of various literacies, skills and procedures requires that a child sees relevance in those things for their own lives. However, what is really needed is much more than the perception of a merely practical relevance. A child must also sense a relevance to something in their inner core, to their deeper wisdom and guidance. This is why self-selection of real-world projects is preferable and, in any case, genuine ownership and engagement are essential.

In the next chapter, we will consider some other kinds of activities and experiences which can help a child to shake off conditioning and learn to experience a deep sense of self-as-connected-with-all-life. We will look at how an education for spiritually conscious living can help a child to feel and trust their intuition, to see things freshly, and to focus their creative energy with intention.

CHAPTER 3

UNLOCKING YOUR CHILD'S GENIUS

The ability to transcend habitual ways of seeing and doing things is crucial to living a spiritually conscious and liberated life. It is so important to be able to let go of what we think we know and be fully present. Let us look at a few more ways in which an education for spiritually conscious living can help a child to shake off conditioning, see things more freshly and deeply, experience a deep sense of self-as-connected-with-all-life, and unlock intuition and creativity.

BEYOND LEARNING
Our usual sense of the notion of education is that it is essentially about learning. However, this has been a mistake. Learning is just the construction of a new pattern of functioning, a new conditioned operating pattern. Learning is just the construction of a new framework for our thinking and our interpretation of experience. Learning has its place, but there is a more profoundly liberating and connecting experience than learning.

Genuinely creative acts and intuitive experiences allow us to transcend and dissolve the limitations of thinking and habitual functioning. They open us up to something deeper in ourselves and the world around us. As we cultivate the experience of quieting the incessant activity of our thoughts and emotions, we find a stillness in our own awareness, a deep sense of Being. And as we get rid of all that static, we become more sensitive to the inner, energetic qualities of things and phenomena around us.

When, from inner stillness, we put our attention fully on a person, a creature, an object or phenomenon, we come into a state of energetic unison with them, and thus are able to intuit their structure and qualities. We perceive and relate with 'true nature' and with the core of other people, not just through the cumbersome and superficial machinery of the intellect. The reality of this deeper kind of intelligence has been recorded by countless people who have chosen not to be

17

bound by the limitations of the intellect. (Some examples are given in Chapter 6, pages 67-69.)

CONSCIOUS EXPRESSION

In Chapter 1, I explained how intimately connected are the processes of our mind, emotions and body. Almost all experience that involves some 'knowledge' or mental component, is part of a conditioned operating pattern that also involves an individual's aims, memory, perception, emotion, judgement, action and biochemical processes and energy flows throughout their body. Significant stuckness or disturbance in any of these components is likely to be reflected in the others. Left unresolved, that stuckness grows—increased mental tension, more closed mind, more distorted perception, more blocked emotions, more dis-ease in the body.

An education for spiritually conscious living will therefore include regular opportunities to release stuck energy. Encourage your child regularly to express their emotions, their experiences, their intentions and their beliefs in kinaesthetic ways, including free form dance movement. Stuck energy is 'shaken out' through such 'deep dancing'. Include sound in these deep dancing sessions. Use a variety of moods of specially selected instrumental and vocal music to accompany and facilitate movement and connection with emotions.

Both within and outside deep dancing sessions, children may also use the voice to get in touch with different qualities of energy within them, and to move it. Encourage your child to make vocal but non-verbal sound to match the thoughts, emotions or bodily sensations they may have. Any sounds. "Ahh, oooohhhh, eeeeeer". They might also use gibberish to express various emotions or what is going on inside. Gibberish is random, spontaneous syllables with no conventional meaning. For example, "pica taka molo ningan wola haly mic". Such non-verbal vocalisation can be particularly effective, since it by-passes the filtering of the intellect and allows deeply felt energies to be contacted, expressed and released. At other times, a child might also use simple musical instruments to express and release what they feel.

Like sound and dance, dramatic expression helps children to get in touch with and externalise their inner life, including their hopes and fears, their joys and yearnings. An education for spiritually conscious living provides regular opportunities for unstructured and semi-structured dramatic play and expression.

In unstructured drama, the child's imagination has free reign. It is a good idea to always have plenty of simple resources, costume elements and props available. You may be invited to participate in such unstructured drama, but your child is allowed to direct. In semi-structured drama, you may suggest or inspire particular scenarios according to your child's interests, circumstances and personality type. The purpose of this dramatic expression is not the cultivation of acting skills as such, and you do not analyse or evaluate your child's dramatic expression according to such criteria. The only suggestions a sensitive parent might make are those intended to assist the child to make a more authentic or complete connection with the emotion, quality or 'energy' they are expressing.

Allow your child frequent opportunities to give visual expression to their emotions, their experiences, their intuitions and their beliefs. The purpose of this artistic expression is not accurate representation or meeting external quality criteria. Such artistic expression is better not accompanied by instruction. Do not analyse or evaluate your child's art work. Do not suggest improvements. Keep your verbal responses brief and observational, rather than evaluative. Should your child expressly request instruction to develop technical skill, by all means provide this if possible, but in a different context.

VISUALISATION

Visualisation is another useful and fun activity that helps children to practice changing and choosing what's going on in their body-mind, so that they are not at the mercy of their memories, emotions and anxious imaginings. Aldous Huxley describes a good example. Here, a teacher invites some children to close their eyes and pretend they are looking at an old, tame mynah bird with one leg, a bird the children are familiar with.

"See him just as clearly as you saw him today at lunch time. And don't stare at him, don't make any effort. Just see what comes to you, and let your eyes shift—from his beak to his tail, from his bright little round eye to his one orange leg."

"...Pretend that there are two one-legged mynah birds. Three one-legged mynah birds. Four one-legged mynah birds. Can you see all four of them?"

They could.

"Four one-legged mynah birds at the four corners of a square, and a fifth one in the middle. And now let's make them change their colour. They're white now. Five white mynah birds with yellow heads and one orange leg. And now the heads are blue..."

…She clapped her hands. "Gone! Every single one of them. There's nothing there. And now you're not going to see mynahs, you're going to see *me*. One me in yellow. Two mes in green. Three mes in blue with pink spots. Four mes in the brightest red you ever saw." She clapped her hands again. "All gone…"

"And now each of you sees three of your mothers and three of your fathers running round the playground. Faster, faster, faster! And suddenly they're not there any more. And then they *are* there. But next moment they aren't. They are there, they aren't. They are, they aren't…"

The giggles swelled into squeals of laughter…[1]

SHHHHH

Opportunities to be silent are very important, too. One valuable silent activity is 'deep listening'. It concentrates attention and opens it to the deeper, vibratory quality of the world around. For example, you can show your child how, with closed eyes, they can note any sounds around them, without getting caught up in labelling, judging or analysing them. And you can sit or lie with them to experience selected music with full attention. Beautiful classical music is best. They do not listen to the music as an object, but put themselves in the place of the music, as it were. What does it feel like to be the music? What is its quality? They listen to what the music tells them. Similar exercises can be done with the other senses also.

Another valuable kind of silent activity has the child passively 'watch' the inflow and outflow of the breath. They just give full attention to the sensation of air passing effortlessly in and out of the nostrils. Point out to your child that they don't have to make the breathing happen. Everything is being done by Nature. To aid focus, perhaps suggest that they gently note 'in', 'out', 'in', 'out', with the flow of air. Suggest that, in that space of quiet noticing, they feel their aliveness. This simple activity helps your child to quieten mental chatter and to cultivate complete presence in the moment.

Another simple activity has your child feeling the sensation of energy in and around their body. They can start by bringing their attention to one of their hands. They will be less distracted by the physical sensation of touch if they position their hand comfortably a little away from the body and other objects. With their eyes closed, and keeping their hand still, they notice their hand. They will probably begin to notice a subtle feeling of energy in and around their hand. If they do, they can open their eyes and notice that they can still sense that energy.

Explain to your child that they didn't feel the energy before, only because their attention was drawn away into the physical world and the mind. Once they locate that subtle feeling, it's easy to be with it. That subtle life energy is the essence of the Life that they are. Point out that the feeling is so subtle that it cannot be truly referred to as a perception, in the usual sense, but a feeling of beingness. "I *am* that energy" feels to be more the case than that "I (subject) am *perceiving* energy (object)."

Now, suggest that your child notices the energy in their other hand. Ask if they can feel some energy in their feet? Their legs? Their arms and chest? What about their lips? Now their face? Next, they can slowly scan their body from feet to head, feeling the inner energy as they go. Finally, suggest that they spend a while, just as long as is comfortable, noticing the field of energy in and around their whole body, homing in on particular areas occasionally, as they feel to.

Noticing the life energy in their body is a lovely way for your child to come into the awareness of Being that is their true self. It is a beautifully peaceful and beneficial practice for them to just sit for a while, noticing the energy of their inner life. When the conditioned mind tries to reclaim their attention with a thought, that's fine. They allow it. It's just a thought: not important and not who they are. They can notice that they are the awareness noticing the thought. Then, they can withdraw attention from the mind again, noticing the energy.

This is something your child can do pretty much at any time, the more frequently the better. They can do it in bed, before sleeping and upon waking. They can do it as often as they think of it through the day. Everything they do that doesn't require a lot of concentration, they can begin to do with their whole being, with some of their attention remaining on their inner energy.

ALLOWING SUFFERING

Becoming more spiritually conscious involves stepping back from the judging mind into formless, observing awareness. One of the most helpful, and ultimately essential aspects of becoming more spiritually conscious is allowing the reality of what is. Being fully present with what is, is not about always feeling good. It also includes being the pure observing awareness that allows pain and negative emotions to be fully felt.

So often, adults try to lessen a child's emotional or physical pain by distracting them from it (for example, "Look at the pretty bird!"), or sometimes by invalidating it (for example, "Stop being so sensitive!" or

"Don't be a crybaby!"), or sometimes by simply ignoring it. But every unacknowledged and repressed pain and emotion is stored in the body and contributes to our spiritual unconsciousness.

When your child is upset, hurt or feeling fear or an unpleasant emotion, encourage them to acknowledge it. Let them know that it is okay to feel it. Perhaps validate them by letting them know that sometimes you also feel fear or pain or negative emotions. They are part of life. Encourage your child to not hide from it or pretend it is not important. It *is* important.

Suggest to your child that they notice that they are the awareness that is noticing the emotion. Suggest that they shift from thinking, "I am anxious," for example, to saying to themselves, "I am the awareness noticing a feeling of anxiety." This will immediately put a little space between your child and the emotion, and assist them in disidentifying from it and just watching it. Then, encourage your child to just sit for a while, and allow the emotion or pain to be there. They fully feel it. They don't think about it, about what caused it or about what the emotion is called or what it means. They just fully *feel* the energy of the pain or emotion. After a little while of feeling it, it will likely ease. But explain to your child that the easing is not what is important. What is important about this allowing or acceptance of the pain or emotion is the allowing and the presence that the allowing awakens—being the pure consciousness that observes what is happening.

FEELING DEEP CONNECTION

An education for spiritually conscious living will also give a child many opportunities to be aware with full sensory attention of their external environment, and of their connectedness to it. This includes opportunities for contact with things that awaken feelings of the magical, and of beauty, tenderness and ethereality. Such things might include babies, baby animals, flowers, fragrances, great art, open sharing of themselves with another, deep listening to another, receptive observation, and regular time communing with nature.

Experiences in nature can be most effective in nurturing a sense of self-as-connected-with-all-life. The elements of nature and its overall grandeur and mystery speak to something deep within us. Being within nature resonates with Being within us, with our essence. It calls that consciousness forth and helps to free us from the illusion of our sense of self-as-separate.

Allow your child to have frequent experiences in nature, of both an unstructured and structured kind. Give them encouragement, time and opportunities to be alone, especially for play and explorations outdoors. Give them ample opportunities to listen, touch, smell and hear of their own volition and without reducing the beauty of that communion to ideas. Allow them to make their own observations and discoveries in nature, without labels, explanations or a limiting focus on outcomes. Depending on the age of your child, there may, of course, be issues of safety to be addressed. What is important is that children are allowed significant psychological space. The key is to ensure that any supervision is *unobtrusive*.

Joseph Cornell developed some very helpful insights into structuring nature awareness activities for children in such a way that their lively energies can be focused on experiences that are deep, subtle and joyful. He calls his approach to structuring and sequencing nature games and activities 'Flow Learning', because it consists of four stages that flow into one another in a smooth, natural and purposeful way. Cornell explains the special value and power of structured nature awareness games and activities:

The strong central current of a river carries away the sluggish eddies that form along the river's banks. Similarly, when you introduce people to nature with playful activities that energize body and mind, the high energy that the games develop washes away personal problems and moods. Freed from personal worries, their enthusiasm and attention can flow into new and fascinating experiences.[2]

The stages of Flow Learning are (1) Awaken Enthusiasm, (2) Focus Attention, (3) Direct Experience, and (4) Share Inspiration. Stage One activities enable you to awaken in your child an intense personal interest. Stage Two activities bring enthusiasm to a calm focus. The focused attention of Stage Two quiets the incessant chatter or static of the body-mind. It allows the child to become more acutely and directly aware through their senses and intuition. In Stage Three activities, the child enters more sensitively into the rhythm and flow of the energy of nature around them, and they experience a deep awareness of their oneness with all life. Stage Four involves the deepening of the inspiration felt in Stage Three through sharing. Your child may share their experiences, and you may share inspiring stories about nature, or stories from the lives of great naturalists and others who have lived with great wakefulness and connectedness. Stage Four sharing strengthens, validates and clarifies the child's own deep experiences.

The broad guidelines of the Flow Learning stages allow great flexibility in nature awareness experiences according to the needs and circumstances of each occasion. The possibilities are endless and the experiences new and fresh every time. There are many books and resources that suggest nature awareness games and activities that parents can include in a Flow Learning approach with their children.[3]

These kinds of nature awareness experiences are also wonderfully effective in creating in children a receptive and inspired mood, prior to scientific, artistic and practical projects and explorations of the world within and around them.

SEEING WITH THE RIGHT BRAIN

Education for spiritually conscious living educates the analytical, conceptual capabilities of the intellect, without stifling the child's awareness of Being, or their capacity for intense non-verbal experience. Different ways of experiencing the world and our relationship with it can be given explicit emphasis.

Huxley describes one effective way that this can be done.[4] The initial object of interest could be virtually anything—a flower, a frog or a spiral nebula. Your child could find a flower that appeals to them, for example. First, invite your child to consider it from a scientific point of view. What does it consist of? Sepals, petals, anthers, stigmas, and so forth. Invite your child to carefully observe the features of the flower, to write an analytical description of it, and to illustrate and label it as accurately as possible.

Then ask your child to let go of thinking, and just look at the flower, not analytically, but passively and receptively. They don't look as scientists, or as gardeners. They try to liberate themselves from all that they think they know about the flower, to look at it as though they had never seen anything like it, as though it had no name or classification. In the way described by Fukuoka, Fromm, Carver, Ellen, Goethe, Alfassa and Burbank in Chapter 6 (pages 65, 67-69), they just look at the flower alertly, but passively, receptively, without labelling, judging or comparing. Your child can hold the flower, too—feel its texture and smell its fragrance, so that they fully engage the senses in appreciating the flower, and fully open with their intentionality to its patterns. Then invite your child to express their experience in words. In its unconceptualised givenness, what is this flower? What does it mean? What does it feel like to *be* this flower? What does it tell you?

Point out to your child that this activity helps them to appreciate the difference between labels and definitions on the one hand and direct, receptive experience on the other, between knowing 'about' things and being intimately acquainted with them. When your child has finished writing, ask them to look receptively at the flower again, then to close their eyes for a couple of minutes. Then invite them to draw and colour what came to them with their eyes closed, whether vague or vivid, just like the flower or very different. Your child then compares their scientific illustration with their receptive drawing or painting, and their scientific description of the flower with what they wrote about it when they were not analysing what they saw, when they were putting aside what they 'knew' about the flower and just letting the mystery of its existence reveal itself directly to them. If you have several children doing this activity at the same time, they can then be invited to share, if they wish, their writings and drawings with another child, and to see that other child's writings and drawings.

You can then extend this activity, if there is interest and it seems appropriate. You can ask your child to consider how all this is connected with what they experience—at home, in nature, in other contexts. When the flower (or whatever) has been considered scientifically and receptively, you might invite your child to look at it in other ways, too. Historically? Commercially? Geographically? Dramatically? Poetically? Practically? What could be done with it, or about it? How could we grow it?

Huxley's activity is a good example of how giving attention to a child's receptivity, deep sensing and intuition can be a complement and antidote to the otherwise alienating training in mental analysis and symbol manipulation. Innumerable variations can easily be devised by a sensitive parent, according to each child's interests, circumstances and personality type. Such activities can lead in a natural way from a focus on an object to a focus on a phenomenon, a person, a verbal or written text, or an event. They draw attention to the interconnectedness, the interrelatedness of everything, including different fields of human understanding and endeavour.

Such investigations may lead to and from not just experiences with 'raw' nature, but experiences with husbanded nature. A valuable feature of an education for spiritually conscious living is the direct participation of children, where practical, in the cultivation of herbs, vegetables and ornamentals, the cultivation of productive and beautiful shrubs and trees, the breeding and raising of a variety of birds and animals, and participation in the life of their community according to their individual preferences, interests and talents.

In the next chapter, we will look more closely at aspects of relationship which are important in an education for spiritually conscious living.

Notes

---

[1] Huxley 1962, pp. 217-219.
[2] Cornell 1989, p. 27.
[3] See, for example, Cornell 1989, 1998; Stowe 2003; and Ward 2008.
[4] Huxley 1962, pp. 211-214.

CHAPTER 4

PRESENCE AWAKENS PRESENCE

In the first three chapters, I have explained how parents and grandparents can provide vital aspects of a child's education, which the technology-that-is-schooling is unable to provide. In Chapters 1 and 2, I outlined the kinds of experiences and activities that parents can provide to help a child to develop important skills and live with deep intelligence, intimately and dynamically connected with the world. In Chapter 3, we looked at some ways in which an education for spiritually conscious living can help a child to shake off conditioning, experience a deep sense of self-as-connected-with-all-life, and live a truly conscious and liberated life.

AWAKENING THE SELF THAT IS DEEPER THAN MIND

More important, however, than the particular activities a child engages in as education for spiritually conscious living, and more important than the physical environment in which most activities take place, is the quality of the psychic or energetic environment. An education for spiritually conscious living cannot be delivered by mind energy, only by the energy of presence.

The mind is certainly a valuable tool for building, in the world of experience, manifestations designed in the depths of Being. But the value of mind is as a servant of our true self. Our mistake has been to identify the self with the contents of the mind, and to think that adding to the contents of the mind can add anything to the self. When we allow the mind to take charge, as in conventional education and the modern world in general, the tail wags the dog.

As we begin to experience freedom from identification with mind, we are filled with an awareness of our true self as peace and oneness with all life. We perceive everything in the world as it truly is, filled with beauty, love and a deeper truth than our intellect is able to fathom. Our uniquely individual expression of talents and abilities comes to reflect a humble creativity that taps the life force power of the universe. Our expression arises, not from mind, but from Being, so that it respects, nurtures and prospers ourselves, others and the world of which we are an integral part.

Each child has their own way of being, their own unique nature and expression of Being. Each has their own life to live. The technology-that-is-schooling is unable to nurture and draw forth that inner life. And in order to be able to sense, nurture and support this depth and uniqueness, parents and mentors need particular qualities and dispositions.

Despite the presence of so many caring and dedicated teachers in conventional schooling, its overtones are nevertheless authoritarian, both in terms of relationship and a commodity view of abstract knowledge. Such overtones are fundamentally at odds with the psychic atmosphere required for an education for spiritually conscious living. What such an education really requires of providers is the wisdom that arises from presence and connectedness, rather than accumulated 'knowledge' and a self that is identified with the contents of the mind. It requires relationship characterised by mutual trust. It requires inspiration, and guidance that deeply respects autonomy and the flowering of the universal within the individual.

RESPECTING INDIVIDUALITY
In providing an education for spiritually conscious living, parents and mentors allow each child to pursue interests which arise from their inner core, because those interests are not arbitrary things. Such interests are expressions of something within the child and, when honoured, allow an unfolding of their life and unique expression of Being.

This does not mean that a parent or mentor should allow a child to do absolutely whatever they want. If a child's interest is in hitting somebody with a stick, to use a very simple and obvious example, a limit needs to be imposed. However, this is not an arbitrary imposition of authority, but an authentic and defensible limit, and these certainly have their place.

The manner of the delivery of the prohibition is most important. It must not be a harsh, authoritarian or threatening "No", which injures the child. It must not be charged with negative emotion. It must be one that respects the person, but places a limit on their action. The two are not the same. A respectful "No" is accompanied by an explanation. This is important, because even a child not old enough to understand the explanation, can feel the energy of love and authenticity behind it, just as surely as they feel the negative emotion behind an authoritarian prohibition. Whenever practical, the explanation comes before the prohibition. This makes the prohibition less jarring to the child. It also allows the child to draw their own conclusion that the action is not okay, before the parent or mentor makes that point.

More generally, in an education for spiritually conscious living, a child needs sensitive and respectful guidance. They do need help in learning to distinguish and reject those thoughts, interests and impulses which arise from conditioning or a sense of self-as-separate. Ultimately, such guidance needs to consist of more than parental authority and power. It means helping the child to feel the difference between a sense of self-as-separate and a sense of self-as-connected-with-all-life. It means helping them to experience how the latter can inform choices and guide the former. Providing such help and guidance, in such a way that it is not rejected, requires something special of a parent or mentor.

EDUCATING YOUR CHILD FROM AN ENERGY OF PRESENCE

An education that awakens a child's deep intelligence, is a deeper level of education than we are used to thinking about. In seeking to provide such an education, the 'knowledge' that a parent may or may not possess is of relatively little significance. As I mentioned in Chapter 1, it will be most helpful if the parent has an understanding of their child's and their own Myers-Briggs personality type. And the parent is preferably fairly accomplished in a wide variety of real-life contexts and interactions, as distinct from school-based genres. But what is of much greater significance is a parent's groundedness in Being. They do need to be relatively free of rigid patterns, definitions and systems. They must be reasonably reconciled to themselves and the world. Parents who can provide such an education are open and authentic, having done away, for the most part, with masks and roles. And consequently, they are capable of intimate connection, of tuning in to a child's 'wavelength', and of evoking a positive response in them. In short, they are people who are themselves spiritually conscious or awakening.

An important feature of education for spiritually conscious living is the substantial 'space' available for talk and listening, particularly between the child and their parent, and particularly as it arises in the context of doing something. Much valuable mentoring is done in such spontaneous focal episodes. To provide this level of education, a parent must be able and willing and have the time to listen deeply to a child. Such a parent will have the inner resources to validate and honour the young individual, whoever they are, to sensitively encourage their uniqueness, gifts, enthusiasms and individual soul expression.

Such a quality of relationship and interaction cannot be nurtured and sustained in mass society. Education for spiritually conscious living cannot take place in institutionalised schooling, where one adult has responsibility for a large number of students. It is a fundamental contradiction. Awakening and resonating with the depths of another person is inconsistent with having to deal with a mass of people. Universality, connectedness and deep intelligence have their place in the dimension of depth, not of breadth. In an education for spiritually conscious living, the child engages, over time, in a wide variety of activities in a wide variety of social contexts and physical environments. At times they may be in a very large group, at a concert or a seminar, for example. At other times they may be on their own. In general, however, one adult can work with no more than a few children, and there must be plenty of opportunities for one-on-one interaction.

OPPORTUNITY

Never has there been a clearer understanding available of how human beings function well, and of the kinds of experiences, conditions and relationships which truly nurture such functioning. Of course, not everyone wishes to see that understanding or to act on its implications. Certainly, governments cannot do it. But some of those parents who resonate with the picture I have painted in this book may wish to do what they can to provide a more nurturing education for their child.

There are many ways and opportunities for each of us to re-educate ourselves for truly conscious living. Any of us who wish to, can cultivate and embrace the sense of self-as-connected-with-all-life, listen to the promptings arising from Being within, and raise and educate our children for a life of greater calm, strength and presence.

CHAPTER 5

WHY SCHOOLS CAN'T PROVIDE EDUCATION FOR SPIRITUALLY CONSCIOUS LIVING

As I wrote in Chapter 1, it is possible to educate children in such a way that they keep and strengthen their authenticity, their creativity, their intuition and their reason. We can educate them to recognise and celebrate the unique beauty within themselves and others. They can keep, into adulthood, their sense of joy, enthusiasm and aliveness. They can keep and strengthen their sense of connectedness, their tenderness and caring, their sense of the magical, and their sense of their own beingness and unlimited capacity. We can educate the young so that they become response-able—able to consciously choose behaviours prompted by a deep sense of self-as-connected-with-all-life, rather than those prompted by a sense of self-as-separate.

Does schooling do these things? No. Our current approach to education treats children as objects, as statistical units. It de-humanises them. It disconnects them from faculties, sensitivities and processes within them that make them 'human'. They lose their sense of stillness, of beingness. They lose their creativity. They lose their sense of autonomy. They lose their sense of relatedness. They increasingly come to feel separate. They come to feel that life is empty and meaningless. They come to feel insecure. They come to feel worthless. They learn to function in 'mechanical' ways, according to external authority, given rules and superficial rewards and penalties.

Why is this so? It is because we allow our consciousness to be dominated by our intellect. When we do so, we experience and view the world in a particular way. We deal with it in a particular way. Most people on the planet right now, especially those involved with education of the young, not only allow the domination of the intellect, they celebrate it! They aspire to it. They advocate it. Our current approach to education of the young reflects the view of the world given us by the intellect.

What is that view? It is the perception of separateness. The intellect

31

seeks to comprehend or interpret the world by *perceiving and choosing between differences*. It arises from and perpetuates a way of being *'in'* the world, but experiencing the self as *separate* from the world. Reliance on the intellect appears to offer us some certainty, some control, some security. The intellect allows us to know something *about* the world, but only in an abstract, interpretive way, as something external and alien. We 'know' things and relate to them as abstractions, as objects of generalisations—by labels, categories and definitions.

Yet, we can provide educative experiences that help children to engage all the faculties of their consciousness as they live *'with'* the world. We can educate them so that their perception and experience of the world is not dominated by the constructions, limitations and distortions of the discriminative intellect, not dominated by rigid patterns of memory, definitions, expectations and judgements. They can know people, objects and phenomena freshly, by a delicate but profound relatedness or identity with them. We can help them to live with deep intelligence, intimately and dynamically connected with life. What a world it will be, when we do! What a world it will be, when we take the lid off humanity. What tears of joy we will shed, when our way of educating children helps them to live with deep intelligence, in harmony with the universe.

As it is, the mass of humanity lives, in varying degrees, in an alienated mode of being, dominated by a sense of self-as-separate. The prevalence of this mode of existence has produced soulless governments, institutions and organisations characterised by a bureaucratic spirit—where human beings are administered as things.[1] Not all individuals who work in bureaucratic institutions are uncaring, or deeply grounded in an alienated mode of being. Far from it. Nevertheless, the bureaucratic spirit and the efforts at control that flow, ultimately, from the prevalent experience of separateness, pervade schooling and society. They manifest themselves in several particular, but interrelated ways.

In our mostly well-intentioned efforts to educate the young, our sense of separateness and desire for control reflect and perpetuate a mental view of intelligence. Recent recognition by some that intelligence has multiple aspects has done little to change the static, commodity view of knowledge that lies deep within the culture of schooling. We seek, through the technology-that-is-schooling, to transfer as much knowledge as we can to the young. In recent decades, there has been fairly widespread acknowledgement that human beings do not just passively absorb 'knowledge', or receive it into an empty 'container'. Accordingly, the talk in education circles has moved from an almost exclusive focus on 'teaching', to a more common reference to issues of 'learning and teaching'. Nevertheless, the nature of curriculum, and the activities and practices of schooling are fundamentally unchanged. The focus remains on compulsory, same-for-all, closed-ended, fragmented, atomised and tightly sequenced syllabus content, objectives or outcome statements.

The technology-that-is-schooling serves the essential control function of ranking young people.[2] Formulations of curriculum serve the more essential function of assessment practices that allow for quantification and comparison of the 'knowledge' acquired by each individual, school, state and nation. Such ranking is seen, by those with a strong sense of self-as-separate (including school-as-separate, state-as-separate, nation-as-separate) as an essential control mechanism for achieving image, status and security.

The so-called educative function of schooling also has a 'hidden' curriculum. The very nature of the experience of schooling has an influence on each child over and above the explicitly stated content and intentions of the formal curriculum. As described above, the effect of that hidden curriculum is to create or reinforce a sense of self-as-separate. The technology-that-is-schooling perpetuates the cycle of the alienated mode of being.[3]

Our sense of separateness and desire for control have vital implications for the nature of relationships with others. The technology-that-is-schooling necessarily involves a bureaucratic approach to the management of its young participants. They are ultimately abstract elements within a massive system that demands rule-bound order, conformity and quantification. Young human beings are administered as things.

Schools are characterised by coercive management of the lives and behaviour of children, by a deep lack of respect for the individual human being. In most parts of the world, attending school is not a choice given to children. They are forced to attend. Then, for ten or twelve of their formative years, children are told in school what they must know, what they must do, and what they must not do. Most schools even force children to do school work at home in the evenings. Limited rewards are offered, mainly in the form of good grades. A variety of penalties, such as detention, are frequently imposed, when children do not comply with demands made of them. Those children who are willing to accept the rewards, submit to playing the schooling game. They learn to do what is expected and work hard[4], and to give the required answers, even when they do not understand them, or the process of reaching them.[5] Those who do not accept, or have difficulty achieving the limited rewards on offer, sooner or later tune out[6], lash out[7] or drop out.[8]

The authoritarian approach to relationships in schooling violates children's autonomy in other significant ways, too. The technology-that-is-schooling denies children the opportunities of significant self-direction, choice of aims and choice of responses.[9] It denies them significant opportunities for the productive use of their own powers. The consequence is the significant atrophy of children's powers.[10] They become 'domesticated'. They develop a learned dependence and a sense of security in conformity. They learn an alienated, symbiotic form of relatedness, sometimes submitting to domination, sometimes dominating others.[11] Deep within the technology-that-is-schooling, bureaucratic beliefs and practices concerned with controlling the behaviour of children perpetuate the cycle of alienation.

Our efforts to educate the young are often justified as preparing them to be able to get a good job, and to strengthen the state or national economy. Again, our sense of separateness and desire for control lead to a particular view of life. A consciousness dominated by a deep sense of self-as-connected-with-all-life has an overwhelming sense of security, of limitless creativity, of faith in its own powers, and of the reality of abundance. However, a consciousness dominated by a deep sense of self-as-separate will have an overwhelming sense of vulnerability, and will posit or accept as the fundamental principle of economic life the perceived 'reality' of scarcity. As the mass of humanity currently lives in the alienated mode of being, dominated by a sense of self-as-separate, this is the position of modern economic theory and of modern schooling practices. In the technology-that-is-schooling, young human beings are reduced to potential resource units. The commodity to be valued, won and accumulated is 'knowledge', especially knowledge converted into the currency of good grades. In coming to feel themselves to be a mere resource unit, children lose their sense of beingness.

A deep acceptance of a scarcity view of economic life leads to a materialistic character structure pre-occupied with acquisition, possession and consumption. Such an orientation leads to competitive behaviours intended to secure and maximise self-interest. Actions, statements and perceptions that might threaten job and economic security are avoided at all costs. Fear of making a mistake, or being seen to have made a mistake, suffocates creativity. A bureaucratic, marketing approach to being in the world seems to maximise the possibilities of 'looking good', of being in demand, of being rewarded. Security is found in submission and loyalty to bureaucratic and intellectual rules, rather than to the dictates of the human spirit, rather than to the promptings that might be felt in a consciousness possessed of a deep sense of self-as-connected-with-all-life. This prevalent orientation of commodity accumulation is based on a belief in scarcity, on fear, on a sense of self-as-separate (and nation-as-separate). It leads eventually to the dissolution of the bonds of human solidarity and to perpetuation of the cycle of alienation.

Around the world, governments spend billions of dollars each year on improving the quality of education. Every educational 'reform' effort makes a government and/or its proponents look good. Education is one of the most used and valued political footballs. Everyone thinks education is important. Any government, organisation or individual who trumpets an educational reform wins great favour, so long as they employ the 'right' rhetoric.

The reforms that win the greatest approval are those that leverage the most popular slogans and images of the time, but, importantly, leave things fundamentally unchanged. A currently popular slogan, for example, is that school reforms will make our state or nation more competitive in the new, global knowledge economy. Governments are using children as pawns in a game of gaining greater status in the global economy through superior achievement of quantifiable educational outcomes. This game has not helped workers to actually be more creative, or intelligent, or fulfilled, or genuinely productive. Such rhetoric only achieves an appearance of value, an image of quality, a pretence of superiority.

The history of school reform over the past century or more shows that schooling has remained fundamentally unchanged.[12] It has rarely led to any significant improvement in educational outcomes. Why? Because these efforts do not question the mistaken assumptions underlying school education that are holding humanity back. They do not fundamentally change the technology-that-is-schooling. They do not address the illusion that we can control other people without dire consequences. And they do not address the alienating illusion of the commodity view of knowledge. In short, they do not confront the issue of our experience of separateness, let alone propose an adequate solution.

Liberating and empowering reforms will not be seriously championed by those accountable for controlling large numbers of people, for improving quantifiable student performance relative to other schools, states and nations. The arguments for student-centred curriculum and educational paradigm change contradict and eventually erode the very reason for the existence of bureaucratic education systems. Despite periodic rhetoric at all levels regarding a shift to a more flexible and student-centred paradigm, when push comes to shove, bureaucratic and political imperatives over-ride evidential, ethical and humane ones.

When referring to conventional schooling, I have repeatedly used the phrase, 'the technology-that-is-schooling'.[13] I have done this to emphasise that the current organisation of schooling is inseparable from the bureaucratic and intellectual values upon which it is built: separateness, abstraction, quantification, control, competition, ranking and a commodity view of knowledge. The necessary changes to the education of children cannot be formulated as "school reforms". They cannot be achieved by adjustments to the technology-that-is-schooling, no matter how large such attempted adjustments are.

Governments and bureaucracies cannot, by their general nature, deliver the emancipatory approach to education, the paradigm change, that humanity now needs so desperately. Anybody who wants a saner world needs to ask deeper questions about our education of the young, and how it can unlock each individual's powers, instead of locking them up. Our experience of the world can be fundamentally different. Education is out of control, in the sense that it is not guided by the mountain of evidence about how human beings function well. Rather, it reflects bureaucratic, political and intellectual values and interests, based on a narrow and distorted, albeit common way of seeing the world.

The most essential change in our approach to educating the young is for adults in general, and governments in particular, to step out of control of the young. Instead, we must help children to deliberately manage the creative power of their own consciousness in fulfilling ways. Managing all our faculties of consciousness to live with deep intelligence, spiritually conscious, is a fundamentally different way of being to the alienated mode of separateness and abstraction. It requires the fundamentally reconceived form of educative experiences I have sought to outline in this book.

Notes

[1] See, for example, Fromm 1976, pp. 148-49, 185-87.

[2] Julia Atkin, identifies some of the practices adopted to make schools more efficient in serving the 'political purpose' of ranking: 'curriculum content shaped by preparation for University requirements; streaming; norm referenced assessment; ranking; learning driven and shaped by written assessment...; judgements of worth having to be objective and quantifiable...; and "League" tables comparing school performance on formal assessment and equating school success with performance on public exams' (1999, p. 7). Elliot Eisner observes that, 'More than what educators say, more than what they write in curriculum guides, evaluation practices tell both students and teachers what counts. How these practices are employed, what they address and what they neglect, and the form in which they occur speak forcefully to students about what adults believe is important' (1991, p. 81).

[3] William Pinar refers to the 'hidden' curricular impact of schooling as the 'disconfirmation' of the child—dependence on authority, obedience to duty, separation of feelings and moral concerns, seeing oneself and others as objects, lack of trust in one's own power. 'We graduate, credentialed but crazed, erudite but fragmented shells of the human possibility', observes Pinar (1975/2000, p. 381). 'What we call "normal"', wrote R.D. Laing in *The Politics of Experience*, 'is a product of repression, denial, splitting, projection, introjection and other forms of destructive action on experience... The "normally" alienated person, by reason of the fact that he acts more or less like everyone else, is taken to be sane... The condition of alienation, of being asleep, of being unconscious, of being out of one's mind, is the condition of the normal man. Society highly values its normal man. It educates children to lose themselves and to become absurd, and thus to be normal' (1971, pp. 23-24).

[4] John Loughran and Jeff Northfield, for example, reported on an action research study that found students have 'well-formed perceptions of the personal and institutional demands of school... Doing what is expected and working hard are the predominant values' (1996, pp. 89, 126).

[5] A study of the interrelationship between thinking styles and learning showed that those students who achieve highest academically are actually those who prefer to work individually, who show adherence to existing rules and procedures, and who do not enjoy creating, formulating and planning for problem solution (Cano-Garcia & Hughes 2000, p. 413). However, it is highly significant that the researchers confirm that, 'As outlined by many educational researchers in the UK, Sweden and Australia, it is untenable to think that students possess inherent, invariant learning styles, or that learning is a decontextualised process... Schools reward with good grades those

students who assume an orientation towards merely reproducing the meaning of learning materials' (pp. 424-425). Paul Black and J. Myron Atkin also report that students prefer to follow rules and procedures they have been given like recipes, rather than developing their own and reflecting on learning (1996, p. 90). And Paul Ramsden notes that there is a 'depressing litany' of studies that constitute a huge body of data with an unambiguous message, that students who 'pass examinations successfully', are 'highly adept at very complex skills', and can 'reproduce large amounts of factual information on demand... are unable to show that they *understand* what they have learned' (1988, p. 14). Commenting on a particular case to illustrate a general phenomenon, Ramsden notes that, 'the pupils "learned", with great success, many strategies unrelated to mathematics in order to provide their teachers with what they predicted the teachers would reward (the correct answers)... even though the child did not understand the process of reaching them' (1988, p. 17).

6 Take the acquisition of language skills as an example. Trevor Cairney (1987, 1988) has observed that one of the main causes of limited literacy development involves the kinds of literacy demands and practices students experience, and the lack of relevance students see in literacy for their own lives. Pam Green (1998) conducted research to find out what kinds of literacy demands were experienced by ten students in their last year of primary and first year of high school. The study found that in the final year of primary school, 45% of writing involved non-fictional genres, 45% fictional, and 10% listing and labeling (p. 121). In the first year of high school, in English only 12% of writing involved non-fictional genres, 16% fictional, 53% predominantly literal Q&A activities, and 18% copying, filling in the gap and listing (p. 122). Similar proportions were observed in History, and in Science. Green noted that between 50% and 69% of all 'writing' was copying (p. 122). A very similar pattern was found in reading activities (p. 127). It should not surprise us, then, that 'Students across target groups are carrying basic literacy difficulties with them into the middle years' (Carrington 2002, p. 2), and that the middle years of schooling are virtually free from additional learning in literacy (Hill & Russell, cited in Carrington, 2002, p. 20). Nor should it surprise us that Green also noted a dramatic decline in positive attitudes to writing, reading, and school in general (1998, pp. 122, 127).

7 According to Evelyn Field (2007), more than one in six children is bullied at school every week. See also, for example, Smith, Pepler & Rigby 2004, and Marr & Field 2001.

8 The tendency of educators has been to illegitimise students by 'psychologizing' student disengagement and failure (McLaren 1998, p. 210) and 'blaming the victim' (Ryan 1976). However, Robert Sternberg's view of human intelligence, for example, emphasises the purposeful, practical nature of an individual's behaviour in a sociocultural context (1988, p. 65).

Intelligent behaviour in everyday life involves '(a) adaptation to a present environment, (b) selection of a more nearly optimal environment than the one the individual presently inhabits [when the environment does not fit one's values, aptitudes or interests], or (c) shaping of the present environment so as to render it a better fit to one's skills, interests, or values' (Sternberg 1985, p. xi). Young people who tune out, lash out and drop out of schooling may often be demonstrating more intelligent behaviours than we have wanted to admit.

[9] This is so, despite such clear understanding that it is crucial for young people to have freedom to choose meaningful activities, set personally meaningful goals, and achieve them. See, for example, Barrett 1999; Erikson 1965, pp. 246-252; and Sheehan *et al.* 2000. Corey emphasises that, without such opportunities between the ages of six and twelve, young people develop 'a negative self-concept; feelings of inadequacy relating to learning; feelings of inferiority in establishing social relationships; conflicts over values; a confused sex-role identity; unwillingness to face new challenges; a lack of initiative; dependency' (1996, p. 105).

[10] Many researchers have emphasised how crucial it is for human beings to have opportunities for purposeful action. Erich Fromm observed that *'the power to act creates a need to use this power and that the failure to use it results in dysfunction and unhappiness'* (1949, p. 219). And Abraham Maslow concluded that, 'What a man *can* be, he *must* be. This need we may call self-actualization' (1954, p. 91).

[11] Erich Fromm maintains that, in the prevailing, alienated mode of human functioning, 'The dominating person is as dependent on the submissive person as the latter is on the former; neither can live without the other. The difference is only that the dominating person commands, exploits, hurts, humiliates, and that the submissive person is commanded, exploited, hurt, humiliated' (1974, pp. 19-20).

[12] It is common for educators to get a great deal right and still miss the point of school reforms (e.g. Ball & Cohen 1999, pp. 3-4; Goodlad, Klein & Associates 1974, pp. 72-73; Oakes *et al.* 1999, p. 242; Stigler & Hiebert 1999, pp. 106-107; Thompson & Zeuli 1999, pp. 345-346). Indeed, the history of curriculum change shows that little has changed (e.g. Cuban 1984; Deal 1990; Fullan 2001, p. 10; Gerstner *et al.* 1994, p. 3; Glatthorn & Jailall 2000, p. 97; Gordon 1984; Hargreaves 1994, pp. 43-44; Holt 2004, pp. 138-169 ; Hood 1998, p. 3; Sarason 1990; Sungaila 1992, p. 69).

[13] This phrase derives from Steven Hodas, who suggests that there is a close relationship between schools-as-a-technology and, '...the institutional and organizational values of knowing, being, and acting on which the school itself is founded: respect for hierarchy, competitive individualization, a receptivity to being ranked and judged, and the division of the world of knowledge into discreet units and categories susceptible to mastery' (1993, p. 28). Daiyo Sawada and Michael Caley also point to the technological nature

of the values and processes that characterise schooling: 'The school is a more or less well-oiled machine that processes (educates?) children. In this sense, the education system (school) comes complete with production goals (desired end states); raw material (children); a physical plant (school building); a 13-stage assembly line (grades K-12); plant supervisors (principals); trouble shooters (consultant, diagnosticians); quality control mechanisms (discipline, rules, lock-step progress through stages, conformity); interchangeability of parts (teacher proof curriculum, 25 students per processing unit, equality of treatment); uniform criteria for all (standardised testing interpreted on the normal curve); and basic product available in several lines of trim (academic, vocational, business, general)' (1985, pp. 14-15). James Ryan observes that these values, along with other reductionist and mechanistic conceptual and methodological schemes employed to 'furnish an understanding of the present (and past) in order to predict and/or control the future... and control human beings' (1988, pp. 17, 19), have long dominated the field of educational administration, and remain central.

CHAPTER 6

HOW HUMAN BEINGS (CAN) WORK:
A SCHOLARLY RATIONALE FOR EDUCATION
FOR SPIRITUALLY CONSCIOUS LIVING

The wisdom of many traditional and Eastern cultures, based on direct personal experiences, acknowledges our fundamental connectedness with all life. Heȟáka Sápa (Black Elk), elder of the Oglala Sioux, for example, explained that,

> The first peace, which is the most important, is that which comes within the souls of men when they realize their relationship, their oneness, with the universe and all its Powers, and when they realize that at the center of the universe dwells Wakan-Tanka, and that this center is really everywhere, it is within each of us.[1]

Similarly, *Bhagavad Gita* recognises the essential nature of the self as 'That by which all this world is pervaded'.[2] It is in the nature of each of us to be able to experience this truth for ourselves, to discover who we truly are.

Such wisdom warns us of the limitations and distortions of the rational processes of the intellect. The *Lankavatara Sutra*, for example, explains that:

> Those who vainly reason without understanding the truth are lost in the jungle of the Vijnanas (the various forms of relative knowledge), running about here and there and trying to justify their view...
>
> The self realized in your inmost consciousness appears in its purity; this is... not the realm of those given to mere reasoning.[3]

A crucial principle of this insight into human nature is, as the Japanese Shih-t'ou Hsi-Ch'ien pointed out, that, 'You won't understand it until you have [experienced] it'.[4] 'Behold but One in all things,' advised the Indian Kabír, 'it is the second that leads you astray.'[5] And the Chinese Lao Tzu observed that, 'The more you know, the less you understand'.[6]

Such wisdom has been less often acknowledged in modern Western culture. During the Middle Ages, religious authority was the arbiter of truth. From the mid-seventeenth century through the eighteenth century, Western philosophy and culture experienced a, so-called, Age of Enlightenment. It aspired to a limited freedom from religious authority, and advocated reason as the primary source and legitimacy for authority in the material realm.

Philosopher and scientist, René Descartes, for example, was a very influential figure of this period. Descartes was an ardent Catholic. He accepted the church's infallibility, and expressed a belief that it must be compatible with his cosmology.[7] However, the church immediately burned Galileo's books suggesting that the Earth moves around the sun, and it publicly condemned those who defended Galileo. Descartes was so fearful of similar censure by the church, that he burned and suppressed some of his own writings, 'since I would not wish for all the world to publish a discourse in which the least word was disapproved by the church'.[8] He courageously applied reason to an understanding of the 'external' world, in a search for certainty.

The 'internal' realm of mind, emotions and soul was much more emphatically within the jurisdiction of religious authority. Rather than noticing that, "Since I am aware of thought, I cannot be the thought", Descartes identified with thought and famously declared, "I think, therefore I am". 'But', he admitted, less famously, 'I do not yet sufficiently understand what this "I" is that now necessarily exists'.[9] He deduced that all things, including the 'I', are perceived 'by the intellect alone'.[10]

Given the backdrop of oppressive authority, even the advocacy of the limited authority of reason was a major step forward for humanity. Its consequence, however, was that, for the next couple of centuries, the emphasis of Western science and philosophy was on intellectual analysis of the external world, through its fragmentation into simpler components for analysis and control. The intellectual search for certainty eased the tormenting sense of vulnerability people experienced as separate, independent units, and enabled them to feel more safe and secure in their environment.[11]

This rational orientation to the world generated apparent material prosperity and tremendous cultural momentum. As the world got 'smaller', the rational orientation began to overshadow the wisdom of traditional and Eastern cultures, and to draw them into the powerful current of its cultural stream.

It was accepted by many, East and West, that the world around us has fixed characteristics that we could come to know. It was widely believed that human beings could discover 'facts' about the outside world that are exact and certain. The main method of discovering 'factual' knowledge was seen to be the immediate experience of our five physical senses, or the use of scientific instruments that extend the reach of these senses. The relationship between human perception and the world was seen as a simple process of undistorted observation of the 'facts' of reality, a view referred to as 'naïve realism'. Logical reasoning about facts was also seen by many to have an important role.[12] It was believed that our perceptions of the world, of these 'facts', which were determined by *the way things are*, could then be simply represented by language as true knowledge.

In this view, knowledge, once 'discovered' and represented by language, is an objective, authoritative copy of reality, a 'thing', a commodity, that can be passed on from one person to another. It can be accumulated. We can learn about the world, without needing to experience it. It was concluded by many adults that, before the young can be trusted with any significant autonomy, we must ensure that they have accumulated enough authoritative knowledge to be able to use their minds rationally and shape their lives responsibly. Some influential educational philosophers believed that certain knowledge claims can be demonstrated as true, and only this 'true' knowledge has a legitimate place in school curricula.

Paul Hirst, for example, argued that all experience is structured conceptually, by the intellect.[13] We then articulate these concepts by means of symbols, particularly language. Hirst argued that the symbols become 'objective' when people learn to use them in the same manner, when an assumed public 'sharing' of concepts takes place.[14] Somehow, this makes the concepts 'true'. Symbols thus derived from experience, Hirst argued, can then be used as criteria of objectivity to test assertions derived from subsequent experience, to determine if they are true or false, valid or invalid.[15] Knowledge from the sciences, the humanities and the arts, thus determined as true, and neatly packaged in discrete school subjects or learning areas, should therefore be the substance of a 'liberal education' of the young.

We should prepare the young for a successful life by teaching them to understand our symbol systems, goes the reasoning. We should teach them our language, expose them to language, both written and oral, and engage them in linguistic interaction. We can identify all the most important truths that have been 'discovered', and teachers can accumulate them in specialised subject areas. The young can then learn about the world by hearing about it, by reading about it, by discussing, reasoning and writing about it. Knowledge can be made a substitute for reality, a substitute for direct experience in the world and for acting on the world.

The reader may be thinking that this all sounds reasonable enough. Indeed, this way of thinking about knowledge and education is still shared by most people, including most teachers and education academics, and is still a major feature of the technology-that-is-schooling. However, throughout history there have been those who saw the inadequacy of this view of knowledge and education. It is deeply flawed on several grounds. Let us see why.

PERCEPTION IS A CONSTRUCTIVE PROCESS
The idea that knowledge is a representation of the world-as-it-is is based on a perceived 'reality' of separateness, on a false dualism of self and not-self, of individual and environment. It is based on a mistaken assumption that there is an 'out there', completely independent of the observer 'in here'. However, such is not the case. Sensory perception is a constructive activity, in at least two senses.

We Select What We Perceive
First, we actively *choose* to perceive certain things, and not others. Some years ago there was an excellent practical illustration of this phenomenon presented on the *Sleek Geeks* television program.

The studio audience and viewers at home were invited to watch a short video clip.[16] The video showed two basketball teams, one dressed in black, the other in white, and each team had a basketball. Members of each team were passing their ball only to members of their own team. Viewers were asked to count how many times members of the white team passed the ball to each other. Rising to the challenge, and determined to be right, I watched closely. I counted 24 passes. After the showing of the video, the TV presenters asked members of the studio audience to reveal how many passes they had counted. Several raised their hands for 22. Several more for 23. Most hands were raised by those who had counted 24 passes. The presenters congratulated these people on observing the correct number of passes. I felt chuffed with pride at my acute observation skills.

Then, one member of the studio audience said that he had seen a gorilla. The presenters showed their surprise at this observation, gently teased the person a little, and asked if any others in the studio audience had seen a gorilla. None had. Nor had I. The presenters then replayed the video clip, emphasising that it was the identical clip to the one just shown. Lo and behold! There, dancing around amongst the two teams of basketball players, was a person dressed in a black gorilla suit! Like most people in the studio audience, I had been focused on counting, and on the activity of things white. Consequently, I had not consciously registered the presence of a shape which was both unexpected and black. Suddenly humbled, I smiled at such a dramatic illustration of how people perceive selectively, according to interest and expectation.

This phenomenon is one of several ideas central to Jean Piaget's insights regarding human learning and knowing. He referred to it as 'assimilation'. Assimilation[17] means 'treating new material *as an instance of something known*', so that, 'when an organism assimilates, it remains unaware of, or disregards, whatever does not fit into the conceptual structures it possesses'.[18] Experimental evidence has even shown that people can shift their focus of attention *within the perceptual field*, without physically moving their eyes or their bodies.[19] We are selective in what we attend to, according to our interest.

Even scientists, who we most tend to think of as impartially basing their conclusions on all the reliable evidence before them, are selective in their perceptions. In his famous work on scientific theory change, Thomas Kuhn found that, in practice, 'normal science', science consistent with the dominant theories and views of the day, 'often suppresses fundamental novelties because they are necessarily subversive of its basic commitments'.[20] Other studies have shown that scientists tend to dismiss findings contrary to a dominant theory,[21] research reports and literature reviews consistent with dominant views are more likely to be accepted for publication,[22] scientists prefer strategies designed to confirm rather than to contradict a theory or hypothesis,[23] and, when research methods permit scientists to attribute contrary findings to measurement error, they have typically done so.[24]

We Interpret What We Perceive

The second sense in which sensory perception is a constructive activity is that we interpret the signals that we receive through our physical senses. This understanding is illustrated by Heinz von Foerster's Principle of Undifferentiated Encoding. 'The response of a nerve cell does *not* encode the physical nature of the agents that caused its response. Encoded is only "how much" at this point on my body, but not "what"'.[25] Thus, signals received by our physical senses represent the *intensity* of stimuli, but the *quality* of the stimuli is not encoded. The picture of the world that an individual constructs from relationships between perceptual signals is an *interpretation*. Understanding that we interpret what we perceive leads us to ask what determines the interpretation each of us gives to our perceptions.

Around the middle of the twentieth century, it began to be quite widely acknowledged that all observations and reports of raw data and 'facts' are influenced by our assumptions, conceptual structures, expectations, goals and preferences.[26] Norwood Hanson illustrated this point by reference to, amongst others, the well-known gestalt image which can appear to be either an old woman or a young woman.

Hanson also cites an example from the history of science, when observation failed to resolve a dispute between Kepler and Tycho as to whether the sun orbits the earth, or vice versa:

> Tycho sees the sun beginning its journey from horizon to horizon... circling our fixed earth. ...Kepler's visual field, however, has a different conceptual organization. Yet a drawing of what he sees at dawn could be a drawing of exactly what Tycho saw, and could be recognized as such by Tycho. But Kepler will see the horizon dipping, or turning away, from our fixed local star. The shift from sunrise to horizon-turn is... occasioned by differences between what Tycho and Kepler *think they know*.[27]

Kuhn emphasised that even scientists' perception and theory-building are influenced by concepts and theories that they are exposed to and accept in the course of their scientific training and professional life.[28] In his landmark book, *The Structure of Scientific Revolutions*, Kuhn showed that scientists do not operate in the ways it had been (and still is) widely assumed.[29] He noted, for example, that two or more groups of scientists can find themselves supporting logically incompatible theoretical explanations for the same set of data. Kuhn questioned the assumption that science can discover and represent the world-as-it-is. He emphasised that scientists do their work and interpret their data within a particular paradigm, a particular set of assumptions or beliefs about the world, or some segment of the world.

THE ROLE OF LANGUAGE

Recognition that our 'knowledge' of reality is greatly influenced by 'what we think we know' changed the way many people view reality, our knowledge of it, and the role of language. Language had been viewed as the expression we give to our perceptions of the world, which were thought to be *determined by the way things are*. A different view came to be widely accepted, which assumed that *language determines our perceptions* of the world. This shift is sometimes referred to as the 'linguistic turn'. This social constructivist or social behaviourist view argues that the gaining of knowledge is mostly a process of transmission through language.[30] Our perceptions, thoughts, emotions and behaviour are believed to be determined, via language, by the social institutions to which we belong, particularly as we are growing up.

This view held that the behaviour of human individuals is purely a response to stimuli in the environment.[31] It held that people are things controlled or completely determined by our environment, including other people. Notions of mind, meaning, feeling, understanding and autonomy were considered 'pre-scientific', 'mentalistic', 'miraculous' 'fictions'.[32] I refer to this view using the past tense, because so much evidence has emerged to show its inadequacy. However, the formal schooling that most of us have experienced was dominated by this view. It continues to be a dominant element of the technology-that-is-schooling. It is reflected in the continued emphasis on externally determined, fragmented, hierarchically sequenced, language-based curriculum content, and various forms of external control, reinforcement and quantifiable evaluation.

However, the view that language is something independent of individual interpretation is a mistaken one. The idea that language is a meaning-conveying structure that all people within a linguistic community share, parallels the error of believing that we can have knowledge of a reality existing objectively, outside us, without our involvement. Meanings (ideas, significances, emotions, memories) do not lie objectively in language elements and structures. Ferdinand de Saussure, for example, explains what happens when two people speak to each other:

> Suppose that two people, A and B, are conversing with each other. Suppose that the opening of the circuit is in A's brain, where mental facts (concepts) are associated with representations of the linguistic sounds (sound-images) that are used for expression. A given concept unlocks a corresponding sound-image in the brain; this purely *psychological* phenomenon is followed in turn by a *physiological* process: the brain transmits an impulse corresponding to the image to the organs used in producing sounds. Then the sound waves travel from the mouth of A to the ear of B: a purely *physical* process. Next, the circuit continues in B, but the order is reversed: from the ear to the brain, the physiological transmission of the sound-image; in the brain, the psychological association of the image with the concept. If B then speaks, the new act will follow—from his brain to A's—exactly the same course as the first act and pass through

the same successive phases…[33]

The association of particular meanings with a word or more complex piece of language is a psychological process that takes place *within* each individual.

Each person's past experiences and their goals are unique, and the word-meaning associations one person constructs will vary in subtle or substantial ways from those constructed by others, even within the same social group or linguistic community. We may share certain understandings and meanings for words to the extent that most of the time we know well enough what each other is saying or meaning. In day-to-day exchanges by proficient language users, most meanings do *appear* to be shared by different speakers. However, the appearance of shared meanings is, at best, a high level of compatibility in the meanings we associate with the symbols of language. When language interactions begin to address more subtle or complex matters, differences are more likely to become apparent.

The common observation that language meanings seem to be shared makes it easy to assume that language captures the reliable or definitive 'truths' of reality. Language *seems* to embody knowledge, and the sharing of such 'knowledge' *seems* to be a fairly straightforward process of linguistic interaction between people. However, such is not the case.

Supporters of the assumption that words constitute a world of meaning and truth beyond personal experience often cite Ludwig Wittgenstein in defence of that view. However, Ernst von Glasersfeld notes that,

> Wittgenstein was, of course, well aware that one could think of 'use' as individual and private, consisting in a person's calling up associated experiences. He had mentioned this long before in his notes for students, but he added that there is something occult about this mental capability and that it should therefore be avoided. He hoped it could be avoided by assuming that the meaning of a linguistic expression could be captured by observing the way a social group uses it in their language games… [Wittgenstein] struggled until his death to convert the notion of meaning and truth into a logical certainty, but the final pages of his notebook (1969) show that he did not succeed in eliminating the subjective element.[34]

Supporters of the assumption that language is an objective entity, 'socially constructed' and shared by all members of society, also cite Lev Vygotsky. However, Vygotsky also acknowledged that, 'To understand another's speech, it is not sufficient to understand his words—we must understand his thought. But even that is not enough—we must also know its motivation'.[35]

THE ILLUSION OF KNOWLEDGE

In science, linguistics and other fields concerned with human knowing, recognition of the interpretive role of the observer is unavoidable.[36] Recognition of this role in art and literary criticism may seem less surprising to the reader than its recognition in the philosophy of science. Or perhaps not. Robert Belton observes that people commonly assume that what makes art 'art' is how accurately it resembles something.[37] Even books on art education make suggestions about how teachers can get children to make their works of art more realistic.[38] Belton argues that this assumption about art as accurate representation is the reason the average person is somewhat alienated from art, since over the past 150 years art has increasingly moved away from the 'familiarity and comfort of resemblance'.[39] And yet, it is ultimately observers who interpret art, judge it and determine its purpose.

In the philosophy of science, there is now recognition that the object or phenomenon under investigation is ultimately interpreted by the observer, by scientists. However, this is not taken as complete resignation to subjective interpretation or to the dominant theories of the time. Not all interpretations are created equal. Scientists operate within the field of experience,[40] and mechanisms in the method of science seek to ensure that interpretations of observations retain an essential relation to the object or phenomenon under investigation. Such mechanisms include, for example, setting up controlled conditions, minimising the number of variables in the experimental design, and seeking repeatability. Interpretations of observations *are* just interpretations, and may vary from scientist to scientist according to their assumptions, commitments and habitual ways of 'seeing' things. Yet, scientific interpretations are not arbitrary, or essentially relative. In art, similarly, acknowledging that ultimately it is the observer who interprets art, does not mean that one interpretation is just as good as another.[41]

We see, then, that knowledge of 'out there' is not passively received 'in here', either through the physical senses, or by way of language. The 'knowledge' we typically create in fields of structured inquiry, and which we focus on in schooling, is based on the mistaken assumption and common experience of duality—being 'in' the world, but experiencing the self as separate from the world. We attempt to comprehend or interpret the world primarily by using our intellect to perceive and choose between differences. We treat elements of reality as though they were discrete or separate, only because our discriminative intellect defines them in that way.

It is undoubtedly helpful sometimes, in limited contexts, to label, define, categorise, analyse, evaluate and apply logic to elements of our experience. But we do not 'know' something just because we have named and defined it. *It is an alienating and costly mistake, in formal contexts such as education, as in everyday life, to let labels and definitions dominate our perception and experience of the world.* Such intellectual and linguistic processes reduce the dynamic aliveness of reality to crude abstractions.[42]

In everyday life, the intellect may play a less dominant role than in structured inquiry, though thought probably does not. Either way, meaning is actively built and rebuilt by the individual, in order to organise experience and establish a satisfying relation to the world. Our 'knowledge' is not a copy of a reality supposedly existing objectively outside of us. A map is not the territory. Our 'knowledge' is not only constructed, it is merely an abstract *construction*.[43] We tend *not* to see things freshly, as they are, here and now. We tend to 'see' through our definitions and expectations, through our memory, our emotions and our judgements. We tend to remain unaware that what we think we know about ourselves and about the world is just a mental construction, an empty fabrication—ultimately not real, just a figment of imagination.

THE COMPLEX MATRIX OF PATTERNED HUMAN FUNCTIONING

Each individual's 'knowledge' is only one inseparable facet of a highly complex system, network or matrix of inter-related, goal-directed schemes, game plans, control mechanisms or conditioned operating patterns, based on previous experience.[44] Each conditioned operating pattern involves many facets and faculties of our individuality, which work together in a dynamically integrated way. Our conditioned operating patterns involve action, perception, memory, emotion, cognition, intention, desire and biochemical processes throughout the body. While the intellect may discern, label, define and categorise 'parts' of these conditioned operating patterns for the purposes of interpretation, no real separation is possible. We may be more aware of the mental, emotional, bodily or behavioural aspect of a conditioned operating pattern, but it nevertheless includes the associated aspects.

The selection and interpretation of sensations, objects, words, ideas, events, actions and contexts typically begin with our existing conditioned operating patterns, which include the aims we bring to our activity. This very significant insight has been emphasised in the writings of many researchers .[45]

During childhood, we construct a multitude of operating patterns concerning our identity, beliefs, expectations, and the behaviours most likely to earn rewards and ensure our survival. From our earliest infancy, and even pre-natally, each of us is strongly influenced by patterns of emotion, intent, language and behaviour that we are involved with directly, or perceive in our environment. Our operating patterns are formed and reinforced by our interpretations of our experience, particularly at home and at school. The formation of each new operating pattern is influenced by existing ones.

With each new conditioned operating pattern we create, we conclude, in effect, not just "This is the way it was just now", but "This is the way it *is*". More than this. We come to conclude, "This is the way it *should* be", and "It should not be *that* way". Our thoughts and emotions begin to take on a life of their own. They constantly colour and judge our perceptions to confirm what we have come to believe about ourselves and the world. *We become attached to, or identified with our interpretations of our experience.* We soon lose awareness of our own beingness, of our own presence or awareness.

We spend much of our childhood imitating and playing games, practising the 'game' of life as we have interpreted it, and as we have observed others playing it. We allow our consciousness to become bound by our 'knowledge', our conditioned operating patterns, which are, ultimately, just constructions of 'reality', just tools. As we grow through childhood and into adulthood, the conditioned operating patterns we have constructed from our experience powerfully affect the beliefs, emotions, expectations, goals and judgements, whether conscious or unconscious, which precede and control our behaviour, perception and experience.

The Creative Power of Human Consciousness
William Powers' Perceptual Control Theory, for example, offers a testable model of how human beings function or behave in order to maintain certain reference levels for a wide variety of conditioned operating patterns felt to be crucial to the individual's well-being.[46] Ultimately, people do not control or choose their behaviour. Rather, they behave any way they must so that their perception, or experience,

matches what they physiologically and psychologically believe they should, or would like to, perceive. *They control their perception.*

More recent research in neuroscience and psychopharmacology has clarified some of the mechanisms involved in our individual control of what we experience. Candice Pert and others in her field have shown that, when we perceive stimuli in a new situation that one or more of our conditioned operating patterns (or 'psychosomatic network', in Pert's terms) associates with previous experience, our interpretation of, and response to those stimuli are affected.[47]

Throughout the body there are chemicals, called peptides, which match various states of functioning and emotion—various states of consciousness. Each cell in the body has several million receptors on its outer surface, each sensitive to a particular peptide. Receptor molecules are constantly in a vibrational state. The way the receptor is vibrating, the shape it is in, causes the cell and the whole physiology to function in particular ways. The cell vibrates between several major favoured states, and when certain peptides are attracted and 'bind' with the appropriate receptors on the cell surface, they make the receptors stable, for a period, in a particular conformation or state of functioning.[48]

When we experience anything, a word, event, environment or personal interaction, for example, a whole set of biochemical processes is triggered within every cell, changing the cells' functioning in many ways that correspond with previous states or responses. Memory is stored in biochemical receptors that are not just in the brain, but are on virtually every cell in the body. The perceptual history of each receptor affects how new information flows, so that,

...the circuitry that will be chosen is a function of what came in the past. That's why... we have a tendency towards certain patterns, even things that aren't instincts. Everything we've learned in our whole life, all the emotional conditioning we've had, predisposes us, not just to certain thoughts, not just to certain movements, but even to specific ways that we hold our body—whether our shoulders are hunched in fear, or whether they're standing back, proud and tall.[49]

We attract or create situations, experiences or states that will confirm a belief or fulfil a certain desired or expected emotional state, and satisfy the corresponding biochemical 'craving' of the cells of our body. So profound is the connection between our subconscious, long-term memory, our emotion and our cellular functioning, that Pert argues that our body *is* our subconscious mind.

Robert Merton noted this principle of human functioning, referring to it as the 'self-fulfilling prophecy'. He argued that it is basic to the social sciences, and that 'essentially the same theorem [has] been repeatedly set forth by disciplined and observant minds...'[50] He observed how a belief or expectation, whether seemingly correct or not, affects the way people behave and the outcome of a situation. For example, Merton describes how, in 1932, defining a situation as real caused a thriving bank to fail. Customers of the Last National Bank, having heard and believed a rumour that the bank was heading for insolvency, lined up to withdraw their deposits. Until those customers held that belief, the bank was actually prospering. Once they believed the bank was foundering, they brought that reality about.[51]

Robert Rosenthal and Reed Lawson conducted two interesting studies on the self-fulfilling prophesy involving university students and rats. As a professor of social psychology at Harvard University, Rosenthal issued normal lab rats for each of his students to train to run in a maze. He told half his students that they had been given rats that had been specially bred for poor maze performance, and the other half of the students were told their rats had been specially bred for good maze performance. In both experiments, the rats believed to be better learners and maze performers, performed better.[52] These studies suggest that the mechanisms of creating the experience we expect, of making real what we believe, are both subtle and powerful.

Rosenthal and Lenore Jacobson explored this phenomenon further, in a study involving the teachers and students of eighteen primary school classes from grades one to six.[53] They randomly selected about 20% of the students from each class. They gave their names to the teachers, telling them that a test of academic 'blooming' showed that these students would show dramatic intellectual growth in the academic year ahead. After one semester, one year and two years, student IQ was re-tested. The students randomly labelled 'intellectual bloomers' showed significant IQ gains compared with students in the control group.[54]

Most of us think of the material universe as made up of solid matter, something concrete, static and predictable. We think of matter as having a molecular structure composed of the smallest units of material existence, atoms. But sub-atomic physics showed us long ago that this view is grossly inadequate. Within the atom are various sub-atomic 'particles', which take up a tiny amount of space compared with the total volume of the atom. Material objects that we like to think of as so substantial, are actually almost completely made up of empty space. This might seem curious, but of little consequence since, nevertheless, atoms function and combine in such a way as to give us the seeming solidity and predictability of the material world. But could it be that we experience the world as a solid given, because we believe it to be so? Quantum physics tells us a lot more about what goes on at the sub-atomic level that has profound implications for how we see the world and our place in it.

Atoms are made up of energy, not matter. Everything in our world is vibration. Sub-atomic 'particles' are popping into and out of existence all the time. They exist in what is called a 'super position', a wave or cloud of many possible positions. When it is not being observed, a 'particle' is *in all these positions at once*. The instant we attend to it, it becomes a 'particle' in just one of those possible locations. The world is creative at this foundational level, since every time we observe, there is a new beginning.[55] No longer does it make sense to think of the world as being 'out there', independent of our experience. Quantum physics tells us that individuals affect the world that they experience.

Neils Bohr's 'complementarity principle' suggests that wave and particle manifestations of electrons are not dualistic natures, or opposite polarities. Bohr saw them as complementary properties of what we might call 'wavicles', since their true nature transcends both wave and particle manifestations. *The aspect of the wavicle we 'see', depends on the instruments with which we choose to experience it.*[56] Quantum physicist, Amit Goswami, points out that quantum physics has not completely replaced classical physics. It has just put classical physics in perspective, shown it to be only part of the story.[57]

Japanese scientist, Masaru Emoto, photographed ice crystals through a powerful microscope, and discovered that different water formed different crystals. He and his assistant found that water exposed to the vibrations of classical music resulted in well-formed crystals with distinctive characteristics. However, violent heavy-metal music resulted in fragmented and malformed crystals.[58] Emoto then wrote words on pieces of paper and wrapped the paper around bottles of water. Water exposed to the vibrations of "Thank you" formed beautiful, hexagonal crystals, but water exposed to "Fool" resulted in malformed and fragmented ice crystals. Water exposed to the invitational, volitional "Let's do it" formed attractive well-formed crystals, while water exposed to the authoritarian "Do it!" barely formed any crystals at all.[59] Human thought or intent affects the structure of water molecules. One powerful message in this research is that the vibratory quality of our thought, our intent, our emotional state, our state of consciousness, influences our own body, other people's bodies, and the world around us, since much of the natural world, including people, is mostly water. And *everything is vibration*.

Candice Pert gives some graphic examples. One concerns people with multiple personalities. Their eyeglass prescription can vary from one personality state to the other. 'One personality will be near-sighted. One will be far-sighted. One will be allergic to cats. One will adore cats.'[60] She offers a second dramatic example of the creative power of human consciousness, from the work of psychiatrist and hypnotherapist, Milton Erickson. He gave several flat-chested women the hypnotic suggestion that their breasts would begin to grow. All grew breasts within two months.[61]

The well-known and well-documented Placebo Effect is another illustration of the power of human consciousness to create physical realities of experience, when there is a clear and unquestioned intent or belief, that is, when we have an intent or belief that is not contradicted *by something else that we think we know*. People get better, for example, when they fully believe something has been done to make them better, even though nothing has been done.

Bruce Lipton describes two examples of research demonstrating the power of the Placebo Effect. Dr Bruce Moseley, a surgeon at the Baylor School of Medicine, conducted a study of patients receiving surgery for severe knee pain. For one group of patients, Moseley shaved the damaged cartilage in the knee. For a second group, he flushed out of the knee joint material thought to be causing the inflammation. A third group received a mock surgery, including sedation, incisions, and surgery talk, but no actual surgical procedure. All three groups received the same post-operative care, including a program of exercise. The placebo group improved just as much as the other two groups.[62] Lipton also describes the research of Irving Kirsch, based on data gathered in 2001 from the U.S. Food and Drug Administration under the Freedom of Information Act. Kirsch found that the Placebo Effect could account for eighty percent of the effect of top anti-depressants in clinical trials. In more than half the clinical trials for anti-depressants, sugar pill placebos performed just as well as the drugs.[63]

Who Determines the Experiences We Create?

Our 'knowledge', thoughts and emotions, and the conditioned operating patterns of which they form a part, *are* all constructed by individuals. But, when the functioning of our psychosomatic network is blocked by denial, repression, trauma or 'outdated knowledge', our bodies become 'a waste dump for the molecules of emotion'.[64] We become stressed by the confusion of conflicting information, impulses and choices, and by the chemical processes that underlie them within our bodies. We lose awareness of our own beingness and we become unable to experience each moment freshly, stuck in repeating patterns of thought, emotion and behaviour. When our operating patterns are conditioned, automatic, operating beyond our conscious control, then to that extent we are addicted to the beliefs, emotional states and biochemical cravings that underlie them as search commands.

To the extent that our conditioned operating patterns are constructed and operate unconsciously, without awareness, choice and intent, significant symbols within our culture *do* function as 'a set of control mechanisms—plans, recipes, rules, instructions (what computer engineers call "programs")—for the governing of behavior'.[65] Up to a point, then, the behaviourist and social constructivist view of human beings as socially conditioned is valid. The creative power of human consciousness is profound. But are we all destined to merely spend a lifetime unwittingly creating realities of experience out of conditioned frames of mind?

COERCION AND CONDITIONING

Human beings are extremely susceptible to conditioning, to alienation. Oscar Wilde famously observed that, 'It is tragic how few people ever "possess their souls" before they die... Most people are other people'.[66] And Hans-Georg Gadamer noted starkly that, 'The self-awareness of the individual is only a flickering in the closed circuits of historical life'.[67]

The accumulation of abstract concepts, and 'bodies of knowledge' that we 'buy into', contributes to our conditioning. When we accept language and abstract concepts as givens, when we allow them to dominate our identity and overshadow our awareness of connectedness and our perception of the world, they disconnect and alienate us from objects, the natural world, other people and ourselves.[68] Spending extended periods of time engaging with linguistic, conceptual and technological representations of life alienates us from our very selves. And as we come to see other individuals and the world as abstractions, we create personal and social realities devoid of humanity.

The soulless forms of daily experience common in conventional primary and secondary schooling contribute to the degeneration of children's functioning into rigid and stereotyped patterns of thinking and largely unconsciously controlled, mechanical patterns of behaviour. Conditioned patterns of functioning are likely to be formed when similar tasks are repeatedly encountered under the same conditions.[69] And conditioning is likely to result when thinking and 'knowledge acquisition' are abstract, superficial and divorced from purposeful action in authentic contexts. This obscures impulses and insights that might otherwise arise from the depths of a child's being, and causes many children to become emotionally detached, to push their emotions into the subconscious. As their awareness of their own functioning decreases, so too does their ability to sense their connectedness with the world, to have authentic knowledge of it, and to creatively act upon it. This is especially so when subject matter, aims and tasks are chosen and imposed by an external authority, such as a teacher, or a mandated syllabus.[70]

The constant or frequent concern with counter-control, with how to deal with and counteract controlling influences from arbitrary authority in the external environment, diverts the young individual's attention from monitoring other input.[71] It diverts their attention from internal signals, impulses, sensations and intuitions. And it diverts their attention from fresh external experience. It alienates them from themselves, others and the world. The result is that inner promptings, spontaneous action, fresh perception and creative learning are all inhibited. These processes become over-shadowed by the individual's primary concern, which is how to resist efforts of others to violate their legitimate autonomy, their right to choose their own expression and create their own reality or experience (where doing so does not violate others).

The imposition of arbitrary authority or control may take quite concrete forms, such as requirements to do or not do certain things. A more subtle, but very powerful form that arbitrary external authority may take is judgement. When we are repeatedly subjected to judgement, our expression, action, learning and overall functioning are inhibited. This is especially so if judgement is associated with reduction or loss of love, approval, or tangible rewards or benefits.

When our receiving of love, approval or other rewards is made conditional on demonstrating or not demonstrating particular behaviours, we learn self-judgement, self-condemnation, and we learn to control our behaviour or functioning in order to win approval and associated benefits, or to avoid winning disapproval. This controlling of our own functioning inhibits our ability to attend to internal signals, impulses, emotions, sensations and intuitions.[72] And it inhibits our ability to monitor the world around us. In short, it may powerfully inhibit our perception, learning, intuition, response-ability and behaviour. It shifts our awareness from presence, from Being, to the goal of winning external approval, and so, takes us out of ourselves.

When stereotypical functioning is externally rewarded or reinforced, through what is evaluated and reported and how, for example, and/or by attaching high stakes to evaluation outcomes, conditioning will become more profound. When spontaneous, creative activity, or making 'mistakes', are likely to reduce external rewards, to meet with disapproval, or to result in tangible penalty, our orientation to the world becomes one of fear, inhibition and defensiveness.[73] Our disposition to engage dynamically with life, and our inclination and capacity to learn through discovering and transcending unhelpful patterns of perception, thought, emotion and action (conditioned operating patterns), are impaired or destroyed.

LEARNING

As we have seen, our perception is typically selective and interpretive. Our system of conditioned operating patterns filters and stores sensory input, and associates it biochemically throughout the body with memories of related experiences. Then, our body-mind activates or suppresses particular emotions and behaviours. This process influences what thoughts rise to conscious awareness. This association of new input with memory is learning.[74] Most learning is the consolidation and elaboration of habitual operating patterns.

Since we tend to ignore material that does not fit into our existing conditioned operating patterns, we might wonder why and how any more significant learning, any significant change in an operating pattern, might ever take place. We often experience a new situation that seems to have similar characteristics to a past situation (though it may also have some different characteristics which we ignore). Such a situation tends to automatically trigger the activity that we have previously learned to associate with that conditioned operating pattern, with the expectation, conscious or not, that we might experience similar consequences. If the result of the new activity is too different from our belief or expectation (if we are unable to assimilate it), then there will be internal conflict and tension. This may be experienced as stress, frustration and disturbing emotions.

Responses to such situations of internal conflict vary from one person to another. Some people may only realise after many fruitless tries, or never at all, that a problem cannot be solved using the same conditioned operating patterns learned in the past. Others will tend to give attention to the new situation and activity, to see if differences between them and previous situations and activity might explain the different result.

If we find such differences, learning may take place as we adjust our conditioned operating patterns, or create a new one.[75] For many complex situations, this will involve formulating the problem in coherent terms and carefully observing the conditions of the situation. Beliefs and emotions previously associated with the situation, by us or by others, are gathered or identified, critically examined, and possibly challenged or reconstructed. In any significant learning, creative and intuitive processes make new connections that move us beyond existing patterns of perception, thought, emotion and behaviour. Solutions suggested by this creative category shifting are applied and evaluated for helpfulness and consistency with the individual's aim (allowing that the individual's aim may also be voluntarily revised in the process).[76]

A similar process may take place when conflicts arise in response to the purely internal processes of thinking. In either case, when we are confronted with evidence that a conditioned operating pattern is not helpful, learning may take place. Any learning occurs in order to confirm our beliefs, knowledge and emotions, to make our conditioned operating patterns more consistent with each other, or to allow for a more helpful or satisfying experience.

Significant learning will not take place if new information has no bearing on our beliefs, intentions or expectations, that is, *if it is not important to us*, whether consciously or unconsciously. Learning will not take place if we do not think the new information is valid. Nor will learning take place if we do not see, or want to see, that new information shows an inadequacy in our existing 'knowledge' or conditioned operating patterns. In such situations we tend to close our minds, and strong emotions of resistance may be aroused. We may even fight 'tooth and nail' to remove or illegitimise evidence that contradicts our cherished beliefs. We saw earlier some examples of how even scientists initially tend to invalidate data or theories which contradict their deeper commitments. This general principle was expressed eloquently in Upton Sinclair's famous observation that, 'It is difficult to get a man to understand something, when his salary depends upon his not understanding it!'[77]

The strength of our identification with 'knowledge', thought and emotion, including all their associated forms and effects, determines our willingness and ability to revise and create our conditioned operating patterns. When learning results in a confirmed, adjusted or newly created operating pattern, it is, nevertheless, merely another construction of the body-mind. We remain identified with and bound by our conditioned operating patterns, albeit possibly new ones.

When we are confronted with an awareness that old knowledge, an old conditioned operating pattern is not working, we often experience a sense of loss, because we have been attached to that old pattern. It has been part of our sense of self. But our thoughts, knowledge and emotions are merely tools, not who we are. What if, instead of quickly drawing a new conclusion, instead of immediately constructing a new operating pattern, we just allow ourselves to 'be' in that 'space'. What if we just be with what is, in that moment, still and fully present? Soon we begin to sense a deeper presence, a deeper reality to our self. Then we are able to transcend our conditioned operating patterns, and open up to something deeper within ourselves, to formless Being.

BEYOND LEARNING

Genuinely creative or intuitive acts and experience allow us to transcend and eventually dissolve conditioned operating patterns. This is a more profoundly liberating experience than learning.[78] It goes beyond learning.

The ability to let go of habitual ways of seeing and responding to things is as crucial in the field of science as in any other arena of human life. There is a paradox regarding the popular image of science on the one hand, and the methods employed by many great scientists, on the other. A great number of scientific discoveries have been initially experienced or apprehended intuitively. In his study of intuition, Tony Bastick concluded that,

> The famous intuitions and millions of other intuitions are responsible for every creation, device, and man-made system of civilization to date. Some might say that it is our reason that has brought civilization this far, but reason is only the servant of our intuition.[79]

The intimate writings of great scientists and mathematicians are characterised by themes such as the belittling of logic and deductive reasoning, abhorrence of the one-track mind, distrust of too much consistency and of all-too-conscious thinking.[80] Eckhart Tolle suggests that 'the simple reason why the majority of scientists are not creative is not because they don't know how to think but because they don't know how to stop thinking!'[81]

Since most people identify with their thought, stopping our thinking is not something we commonly practice in the modern world. One way that most of us have experienced this, if only momentarily, is in appreciating great art. The best art, in any of its many and varied forms, visual, musical, literary, culinary, architectural and so forth, contains some sense of the universal that calms the turbulent mind. It may stop our habitual thinking and provide a release from our conditioned ways of seeing things. Robert Belton clarifies this function by describing three categories of statements about a work of art, namely, Context, Form and Content.[82]

The artist's mode of consciousness, their attitudes, beliefs, preferences, lifestyle and social standing form the Primary Context of the work, whereas the inner and outer circumstances of each individual who observes the work of art constitute a Secondary Context. Form consists of the work itself. Primary Form consists of the elements in isolation, such as colour, light, texture, shape, size and medium in a painting, for example. How these elements are related to each other, as in balance, composition, contrast, distance, perspective and space in a painting, creates Secondary Form.

The Content of a work of art consists of both 'meanings' intended by the artist, and the work's 'significances' for individual observers.[83] The Primary Content of a work consists of people, places, things and events all representing what they appear to represent—a dog in a painting, for example. Yet, one or more elements of Primary Content may be used by the artist to suggest a different level of meaning or significance, a Secondary Content. The presence of a dog in a painting, for example, may suggest faithfulness or loyalty. This will depend on the observer's Contextual codes, and/or on the observer's knowledge of the artist's Contextual codes.

It is not just Context that pushes Content from Primary to Secondary. Form also influences the meaning and significance of a work of art, using a method of category-shifting that Belton refers to as 'paralinguistic', even though the term strictly applies to the use of spoken language. Changes in individual expression, delivery or performance of a message lead to changes in our understanding of what is meant. For example, most fluent speakers of English immediately recognise the difference between the sound and significance of the word 'help' spoken neutrally and 'Help!' shouted desperately. In the context of visual art, then, if one changes the Form of a literal image, that is, the *way* it is represented, the image can be made to suggest a different meaning, or another level of meaning or significance. As an example, Belton points out how the departure from conventional ways of depicting the night sky in Vincent van Gogh's painting, "The Starry Night", evokes 'a deeply emotional response, and the scene almost cries out in mystical ecstasy'.[84]

Thus, truly creative art involves the selection and combination of Form, Context and Primary Content to create Secondary Content, which expresses profound meaning or evokes a deeply felt response in the observer. Rather than attempting merely to represent objective reality, art can help to unlock our conditioned ways of seeing and engaging with the world. It can express a deeper reality that unlocks the soul from its mental prison and, in so doing, it can unlock our own creativity. Art may help to liberate us from the bonds of what we think we know, so long as neither artist nor observer gets entangled in intellectualising it—analysing the technique, the form, the content—but allows the paralinguistic shift to be experienced and felt.

The great value and appeal of humour, too, is that when two previously isolated contexts or conditioned operating patterns collide in a joke, the result is a sense of being liberated from the prison of our judgement-laden and habitual ways of seeing things.

Two men drinking in a bar. After quite a few drinks, one man looks at the other and says, "I think I should tell you, I've been sleeping with your mother". The second man pauses, looks the first steadily in the eyes, and says, "Go home, Dad, you're drunk!"

Another.

A skeleton walks into a bar and says to the bartender, "Er, gimme a beer and a mop".

What about this one?

Two empaths meet in the street. One says to the other, "Hi. You're fine, how am I?"

Or this one?

What are time flies, and why do they like an arrow?

One more.

There was a bloke in Sydney who wanted personalised number plates for his car, but he couldn't afford them. So, he changed his name to TLX126.

In humour, two or more different meanings or conceptual perspectives run into each other and clash. Their assumed 'truth' or 'rightness' is challenged and shattered, and the tension in each is released in laughter. Humour subverts the authority of our ideas. We see them for what they are—merely conditioned constructions of the body-mind. Hence, the proverbially therapeutic effect of laughter.

There are many other ways in which we can still the incessant and binding activity of the mind. We looked at a few of these in Chapter 3. But what is it like, when the clamour of habitual thought and emotion that most people experience constantly is completely silenced? How would we see the world, if our consciousness was not dominated by the experience of self-as-separate? Brain scientist, Jill Bolte Taylor, had an unexpected opportunity to find out, when she had a stroke in 1996. The stroke was caused by a blood clot the size of a golf ball pressing against the language centres of her brain, effectively shutting down the left hemisphere.

On the morning of the stroke, I woke up to a pounding pain behind my left eye…

And I look down at my arm and I realize that I can no longer define the boundaries of my body. I can't define where I begin and where I end, because the atoms and the molecules of my arm blended with the atoms and molecules of the wall. And all I could detect was this energy. Energy. And I'm asking myself, "What is wrong with me, what is going on?" And in that moment, my brain chatter, my left hemisphere brain chatter went totally silent. Just like someone took a remote control and pushed the mute button and… total silence.

And at first I was shocked to find myself inside of a silent mind. But then I was immediately captivated by the magnificence of energy around me. And because I could no longer identify the boundaries of my body, I felt enormous and expansive. I felt at one with all the energy that was, and it was beautiful there.[85]

It took Taylor eight years to fully recover from her stroke, but she treasures the liberating 'stroke of insight' that her experience gave her. She recounts:

My left hemisphere had been trained to perceive myself as a solid, separate from others. Now, released from that restrictive circuitry, my right hemisphere relished its attachment to the eternal flow. I was no longer isolated and alone. My soul was as big as the universe and frolicked with glee in a boundless sea.

…in this shifted perception, it was impossible for me to perceive either physical or emotional loss because I was not capable of experiencing separation or individuality…

Although I rejoiced in my perception of connection to all that is, I shuddered at the awareness that I was no longer a normal human being. How on earth would I exist as a member of the human race with this heightened perception that we are each a part of it all, and that the life force energy within each of us contains the power of the universe? How could I fit in with our society when I walk the earth with no fear? ...there was both freedom and challenge for me in recognizing that our perception of the external world, and our relationship to it, is a product of our neurological circuitry. For all those years of my life, I really had been a figment of my own imagination![86]

Eckhart Tolle had a somewhat similar experience of re-establishing his awareness of self-as-connected-with-all-life. Unlike Taylor's, however, Tolle's experience arose out of a crisis of thought and emotion, rather than of the physical body.

One night... I woke up in the early hours with a feeling of absolute dread... everything felt so alien, so hostile, and so utterly meaningless that it created in me a deep loathing of the world... [and of] my own existence...

"I cannot live with myself any longer." This was the thought that kept repeating itself in my mind. Then suddenly I became aware of what a peculiar thought it was. "Am I one or two? If I cannot live with myself, there must be two of me: The 'I' and the 'self' that 'I' cannot live with." "Maybe," I thought, "only one of them is real."

I was so stunned by this strange realization that my mind stopped. I was fully conscious, but there were no more thoughts. Then I felt drawn into what seemed like a vortex of energy...

[In the morning] I was awakened by the chirping of a bird outside the window. I had never heard such a sound before. My eyes were still closed, and I saw the image of a precious diamond. Yes, if a diamond could make a sound, that is what it would be like. I opened my eyes. The first light of dawn was filtering through the curtains. Without any thought, I felt, I knew, that there is infinitely more to light than we realize. That soft luminosity filtering through the curtains was love itself. Tears came into my eyes. I got up and walked around the room. I recognized the room, and yet I knew that I had never truly seen it before. Everything was fresh and pristine, as if it had just come into existence. I picked up things, a pencil, an empty bottle, marveling at the beauty and aliveness of it all.

...I could still function in the world, although I realized that nothing I ever did could possibly add anything to what I already had.

...More fundamental, perhaps, than any experience is the

undercurrent of peace that has never left me since then.[87]

Plant disease scientist, Masanobu Fukuoka, describes his moment of insight, after being in an agony of doubt about the nature of life and death.

One night as I wandered, I collapsed in exhaustion on a hill overlooking the harbour, finally dozing against the trunk of a large tree... As the breeze blew up from below the bluff, the morning mist suddenly disappeared. Just at that moment a night heron appeared, gave a sharp cry, and flew away into the distance. I could hear the flapping of its wings. In an instant all my doubts and the gloomy mist of my confusion vanished. Everything I had held in firm conviction, everything upon which I had ordinarily relied was swept away with the wind. I felt that I understood just one thing. Without my thinking about them, words came from my mouth: "In this world there is nothing at all..." I felt that I understood nothing.

I could see that all the concepts to which I had been clinging, the very notion of existence itself, were empty fabrications. My spirit became light and clear. I was dancing wildly for joy... Everything that had possessed me, all the agonies, disappeared like dreams and illusions, and something one might call "true nature" stood revealed.

...there is nothing special about me, but what I have glimpsed is vastly important.[88]

We see from these and similar experiences of a sense of self-as-connected-with-all-life *the utter insufficiency of what we think we know with our intellect, with our thinking mind.* Tolle emphasises that such a state is both our own essential nature, and a state of connectedness with Being, which is the innermost essence deep within every form. Since it is our own true nature, our deepest self, it is accessible to us now. 'But don't try to grasp it with the mind,' advises Tolle. 'Don't try to understand it. You can know it only when the mind is still. When you are present, when your attention is fully and intensely in the Now, Being can be felt, but it can never be understood mentally.'[89]

Fukuoka also recognised that others would not be able to understand mentally the nature and value of the awakening of this sense of self-as-connected-with-all-life. He decided to demonstrate it by becoming a farmer. He explains his 'raw personal experience' of farming rice by becoming one with nature:

We must look closely at a rice plant and listen to what it tells us... However, "to look at" or "scrutinize" rice does not mean to view rice as the object, to observe or think about rice. One should essentially "put oneself in the place of the rice". In so doing, the self looking upon the rice plant vanishes. This is what it means to "see and not examine and in not examining to know". Those who have not the slightest idea what I mean by this need only devote themselves to their rice plants.[90]

What is the value of regaining awareness of Being, then, and is it being suggested that thinking has no value? Not at all. The mind is a very valuable tool for building, in the world of experience, manifestations designed by intuitive and creative inspiration. The value of mind is as a servant of our true self. *Our mistake is to identify self with the contents of the mind, and to think that adding to the contents of the mind can add anything to the self.* When we allow the mind to take charge, the tail wags the dog. But, as Tolle explains, in the state of awareness of self-as-connected-with-all-life,

> ...you still use your thinking mind when needed, but in a much more focused and effective way than before. You use it mostly for practical purposes, but you are free of the involuntary internal dialogue, and there is inner stillness. When you do use your mind, and particularly when a creative solution is needed, you oscillate every few minutes or so between thought and stillness, between mind and no-mind. No-mind is consciousness without thought. Only in that way is it possible to think creatively, because only in that way does thought have any real power. Thought alone, when it is no longer connected with the much vaster realm of consciousness, quickly becomes barren, insane, destructive.[91]

As we practice quieting the incessant activity of our thoughts and emotions, and getting in touch with the stillness of our own awareness, we become more receptive to the inner, energetic qualities of things and phenomena around us. A stone thrown into the turbulent, wind-whipped surface of a lake, quickly disappears without a trace. However, even a small pebble thrown into a glassy-still lake sets up a very clear pattern of vibratory ripples. In like fashion, with the usual turbulence of our labelling, analysing, reasoning and judging body-mind, we find it difficult to register much more than the surface values of the world around us. However, when the mind is stilled and we are fully present in the now, we are more sensitive to our inner world, and better able to 'answer' the vibratory resonance of objects, creatures and phenomena around us.

Some years ago, I went walking by a river. My intention was to be fully present with my physical senses, without getting caught up in labelling, conceptualising and analysing. As I walked, I checked in with my sight, avoiding, as best I could, labelling the particular things I saw. What sounds could be detected? What was the feel of my foot pressing against the earth with each step, the feel of my legs against my trousers, the breath of breeze against my cheeks? What smells were in the air? After a few minutes, I noticed a nice view, partly obscured by a dead bush. I thought, "If that bush wasn't in the way, that would make a great photograph. Hmm. I wish I had brought my camera…" I soon realised that I was getting caught up in thoughts, so I went back to checking in with my senses. Before long, I saw a stretch of river ahead, partly obscured by the dead limb of tree. "Wow," I thought, "that would make a beautiful photograph, if only that branch wasn't there." Whoops. I quickly realised that I was again analysing and evaluating my experience, so I refocused on being fully present with my senses. Soon, along with the conventional beauty of nature, I was noticing more 'imperfections' in the scenery, an eroded section of path, a fallen tree, a discarded drink can. But I was less distracted into thought, and better able to continue my sensory attention. After a while, a subtle, but deeply significant realisation came into my consciousness. "*Everything* is beautiful, if I give it my *full* attention."

When, from inner stillness, we put our attention fully on a person, a scene, an object or phenomenon, the vibratory states of our very cells resonate with the vibratory quality of the object of attention. We resonate with the deeper life of which the objects and events are only the outer expression. We come into a state of energetic unison with them, and thus are able to intuit their structure and qualities. We perceive and relate with 'true nature' and with the core of other people, not just through the cumbersome and superficial machinery of the intellect.

The reality and depth of the oneness experienced when this connected mode of being is activated within us has been recorded by countless people who have chosen not to be bound by the limitations of the discriminative intellect. Here are just a few more brief examples of this experience of a sense of self-as-connected-with-all-life.

In his book, *The Art of Loving*, psychoanalyst, Erich Fromm, contrasts the abstract knowledge of the alienated mode of being with the kind of knowledge that makes possible mature love: 'I know in the only way knowledge of that which is alive is possible for man—by experience of union—not by any knowledge our thought can give'.[92]

Botanist, George Washington Carver, who, being a freed slave, never had any formal schooling, noted that, 'Anything will give up its secrets if you love it enough'.[93]

A child, named 'Ellen', described how she is able to open up to an intuitive mode of perception:

There is a deep focus that comes from staring. Then I seem to move into this other, deeper level where I see and know things. We're taught not to stare, but little kids do, and staring moves you into another dimension. I am able to see and understand things in those moments. It's like these images have a wave of intuition that goes along with them. You see them and know their meaning.[94]

The philosopher, Wolfgang von Goethe, observed that,

There is a delicate empiricism which makes itself utterly identical with the object, thereby becoming true theory... Individual phenomena must never be torn out of context. Stay with the phenomena, think within them, accede with your intentionality to their patterns, which will gradually open your thinking to an intuition of their structure.[95]

Mirra Alfassa recalls that she began opening to an awareness of her connectedness with all of life between the ages of eleven and thirteen. One particular feature of this experience of oneness was her ability to sense the distinctive inner qualities of different flowers. She records one such experience:

A deep concentration seized on me, and I perceived that I was identifying myself with a single cherry-blossom, then through it with all cherry-blossoms, and, as I descended deeper in consciousness, following a stream of bluish force, I became suddenly the cherry-tree itself, stretching towards the sky like so many arms its innumerable branches laden with their sacrifice of flowers... [N]ow the blood of the cherry-tree flows in my veins and with it flows an incomparable peace and force. What difference is there between the human body and the body of a tree? In truth, there is none: the consciousness which animates them is identically the same.

Then the cherry-tree whispered in my ear: "It is in the cherry-blossom that lies the remedy for the disorders of the spring."[96]

Botanist and agricultural scientist, Luther Burbank, described the conditions and benefits of this connected mode of being in this way:

Preconceived notions, dogmas, and all personal prejudice and bias must be laid aside. Listen patiently, quietly, and reverently to the lessons, one by one, which Mother Nature has to teach, shedding light on that which was before a mystery, so that all who will, may see and know. She conveys her truths only to those who are passive and receptive. Accepting these truths as suggested, wherever they may lead, then we have the whole universe in harmony with us.[97]

As we engage in a rich and purposeful experience of the material and social world, as we practice the stillness of complete presence in the now, and as we concentrate awareness in the deeper life of objects and events, we are able to receive direct and intuitive knowledge of the world around us and to pour potent life into our creative intentions. We receive and express the inspirations of 'genius' that flash into consciousness from the depths of Being. All knowledge is within us. We are then intelligence become conscious of itself.

Based on their understandings of the biochemical and neurological workings of the body-mind, and on their personal experience, both Pert and Taylor affirm that each person can become conscious of their conditioned operating patterns, and step out of them.[98] We can take more responsibility for managing consciousness, for whether we choose to run the circuitry of self-as-separate, or self-as-connected-with-all-life. Taylor emphasises that,

…we have the power to choose, moment by moment, who and how we want to be in the world. Right here right now, I can step into the consciousness… where we are—I am—the life force power of the universe, and the life force power of the 50 trillion beautiful molecular geniuses that make up my form. At one with all that is. Or I can choose to step into the consciousness… where I become a single individual, a solid, separate from the flow, separate from you. I am Dr. Jill Bolte Taylor, intellectual, neuroanatomist. These are the 'we' inside of me.[99]

The consciousness of every child has a similar 'we', who need acknowledgement and nurturing. Psychologist, Tobin Hart, conducted a five-year research study of children's experiences beyond the narrow consciousness of self-as-separate. He explored their experiences of a 'spiritual world', which he defined as involving an 'intimate and intuitive awareness of the world', claiming our 'shadowy parts', and experiencing self as 'an interconnected spiritual being, even as spirit itself'.[100] Hart found overwhelming evidence that children have a rich and formative spiritual life.[101] He observed that, having lost touch with such consciousness themselves, many adults tend to confuse spiritual life with the abstract, rational activity of thinking and talking about religious concepts. Consequently, adults in general, and researchers and educators in particular, tend to neglect and even repress the spiritual consciousness of children.[102]

DEEP INTELLIGENCE

Despite the almost universal experience of separateness, brought about by our almost exclusive focus on rational processes in schooling, separateness is not the ultimate reality. Despite the claims of the so-called 'Age of Enlightenment', the faculty of reason is not the highest faculty in human beings.

The popular, mental view of intelligence is grossly inadequate. It ignores the existence and significance of a variety of intimately connected human faculties. A more complete experience of human intelligence may be described as *the ability to prosper through connectedness with the world*. The conventional notion of intelligence is about being 'in' the world, but experiencing the self as separate from it. What I call 'deep intelligence' is about living by means of the world, intimately and dynamically connected with it. In the former, we may 'know' about the world, in an abstract, interpretive way. In the latter, we engage all the faculties of our consciousness as we live with the world. Deep intelligence is *our ability to prosper through conscious coordination of the inner and outer faculties of our being with the inner and outer qualities of the world through which we live*.

Education for spiritually conscious living helps children to experience the stillness of their own awareness, their inner essence. It helps them to detach from abstract concepts and programmed patterns of thinking and emotion, to perceive things freshly and more deeply, and to sense the bubbling up of intuitions and inner yearnings. We are, in essence, energy, and all the things and phenomena around us are energy. When we are not full of conflicting energies of thought and emotion, we can deliberately initiate subtle vibrations of intent within the stillness of our consciousness. These vibrations influence the world around us in a creative way, in a way which causes corresponding vibrations to be set up and manifested in forms, phenomena and events that we experience.

What is most notable about Merton's observations, about Rosenthal and Jacobson's research, and about so much related research and observation, is the general failure of educators to recognise the significance *for the aims of education* of the understanding that the thoughts, feelings and intentions of all human beings are creative. Education for spiritually conscious living helps children to find, express and create in their lives those realities that are more deeply satisfying to them, and that are more sustainable and life-supporting.

Giving our experience more conscious attention makes the unconscious conscious. When we allow ourselves to see our conditioned operating patterns, our emotions, definitions, beliefs and fears, for what they are, when we face and experience our buried memories, and our hidden emotions and impulses, we release ourselves from their hold. A mode of perception, knowing and connectedness opens up that is beyond the purely cognitive, beyond the abstract. As people begin to live more 'consciously', all things begin to work in continuity with each other, to flow in a form of unity, in a dynamic and sustainable relationship.

Choice plays an important role in such conscious, 'mindful' living. Choice and fully conscious functioning require that each of us knows our 'self' deeply and fully, including our significant conditioned operating patterns, our selfish impulses, our emotions, reaction patterns and conditioning, as well as our 'inner' perceptions, intuitions and soul urges.

There may be differences between the formulations of what we think or feel we should experience that arise from different areas of our body-mind-soul system. We may have, for example, various conditioned operating patterns involving fears and drives based on the perception of self-as-separate. Others involve learned patterns of thought, belief and emotion associated with the views, mores and laws of those around us—our community, our school, our parents, close friends, relatives and associates. Some of the concepts, beliefs and judgements operating on this 'level' explicitly serve the purpose of over-riding certain ego-based impulses. There will be other operating patterns we have consciously learned (constructed) for ourselves, based on experience and reflection.

However, on a 'deeper' level, there may be promptings or values or motivations that arise through intuition, or some deep sense of inner knowing or feeling. Feelings, perceptions and motivations at this level have a quality of universality, of connection, of self-transcendence. They may contradict the socially sanctioned beliefs and judgements of our conditioning (and of our social group). The irony is that *it is only by respecting, supporting and enlivening consciousness at this deep level within each individual, that each person can experience the flowering of the self-transcendent feelings and intents.* Universality, connectedness and deep intelligence have their place in the dimension of depth, not breadth.

The solution to the dilemma of our suppressed deep intelligence, lies in educative experiences relating to our sense of self-as-connected-with-all-life and to the conscious, but not overly mental use of choice. There are many ways in which education for spiritually conscious living can help the young to manage their experiences, their consciousness, their environments, deliberately to facilitate the shifting of their functioning, their state of consciousness, from their sense of self-as-separate to a sense of self-as-connected-with-all-life, so that the latter informs and guides the former. The objective is not to deny the 'narrower' thoughts, emotions and behaviours, to hide from them, fear them, or feel guilt or shame for them. The objective is to recognise them, face them, and bring them into the governance of the more expansive, universal self, by full awareness and conscious choice. Such surrender of narrow self-interest, challenging of social conformity and arbitrary authority, and obedience to a higher command both requires and cultivates the essence of courage, nobility and heroism.[103]

The basis of our suffering is our identification with the contents of our mind. The basis of our weakness, insecurity, worry, struggle, emptiness, fear of lack and loss, and destructive drives and motivations, is our attachment to learned operating patterns, to our knowledge. But we have within us, all of what it takes to manifest now a very different kind of experience, a different way of being in the world. We can manage all the faculties of our consciousness so that we transcend the prejudice of learned knowledge, and dance in the wisdom of the moment.

As we begin to experience freedom from identification with mind, we are filled with an awareness of our true self as peace and oneness with all life. Our uniquely individual expression of talents and abilities comes to reflect not the mind, but intuition and creativity that tap the deep intelligence of Being.

For civilisation to make a transition from the alienated mode of existence to one characterised, not by the *idea*, but by the *experience* of connectedness, prosperity and cooperation with all of life, all we need do is begin to play the instrument of our whole human 'being'. This requires a fundamentally different kind of education for the young, the general features of which I have outlined in this book.

Notes

1 Black Elk 1988, p. 115.
2 Quoted in Huxley 1970, p. 3.
3 Quoted in Huxley 1970, p. 8.
4 Quoted in Huxley 1970, p. 127.
5 Quoted in Huxley 1970, p. 10.
6 Tzu 2013, chap. 47.
7 Clarke 2006, p. 451.
8 Quoted in Clarke 2006, p. 112.
9 Descartes 1641, para. 6.
10 Descartes 1641, para. 18.
11 It is ironic that this intellectual search for certainty was given such impetus by Descartes, since his own intellectual search for certainty led him to conclude that the only 'true thing' left is, 'Perhaps just the one fact that nothing is certain' (1641, para. 2).
12 Arthur Houts summarises the logical positivist view in this way: 'The operation of logic on "facts" leads to truth; science contains "factual statements" and conforms to logic; therefore, science leads to truth' (1989, p. 52).
13 Hirst 1972, p. 123.
14 Hirst 1972, p. 124.
15 Hirst 1972, p. 124.
16 The clip comes from a DVD, Surprising Studies of Visual Awareness, vol. 1 (2003).
17 Jean Piaget's idea of assimilation is often misunderstood as a process whereby material is brought into the individual *from the environment*. After concentrating almost exclusively on Piaget for six years and periodically revisiting his work for a further twenty years, reading both English translations and the original French writings of Piaget, Ernst von Glasersfeld, a multilingual psychologist and specialist in linguistics, notes that the vast majority of translations of Piaget's writings make it almost impossible to understand his views. This is a consequence, he argues, of the 'naïve realist' philosophical assumptions of translators, which have caused them to unconsciously bend what they read in Piaget's original texts. Moreover, because Piaget's writing is not easy reading, and because of the sheer volume of his work, most of those who seek to summarise his ideas do so

based on a small number of books or articles. Consequently, Glasersfeld argues that countless texts and articles about Piaget's ideas provide an incomplete view of his theory, or distort key concepts (1995, pp. 12, 53).

[18] Glasersfeld 1995, pp. 62-63.

[19] Glasersfeld 1995, pp. 10-11, 116.

[20] Kuhn 1970, p. 5.

[21] See, for example, Arkes & Harkness 1983; Crocker 1981; Jenkins & Ward 1965; Lord, Ross & Lepper 1979; Nisbett & Ross 1980; Quine 1971; Ross & Lepper 1980; Schustack & Sternberg 1981; Shaklee & Mims 1981.

[22] See, for example, Abramowitz, Gormes & Abramowitz 1975; Barber 1961; Glasersfeld 1995; Goodstein & Brazis 1970; Mahoney 1977; Snizek, Fuhrman & Wood 1981.

[23] See, for example, Klayman & Ha 1987. Contrast the common preference for confirmatory strategies with Karl Popper's argument that observing many instances which support a principle does not guarantee that we might not see it contradicted in the future (1959, 1963). Popper argued for an alternative experimental criterion, the principle of falsification, since only one observation at variance with a principle will prove it false (1963).

[24] See, for example, Gorman 1986; Kern 1982; Quine 1971; Tuckman 1974.

[25] Foerster 1981, p. 293.

[26] For example, Dewey 1931; Hanson 1958; Kuhn 1962; Polanyi 1962.

[27] Hanson 1958, pp. 23-24 (my emphasis).

[28] 'Already it should be clear', wrote Kuhn, 'that the explanation [for theory development and replacement] must, in the final analysis, be psychological or sociological. It must, that is, be a description of a value system, an ideology, together with an analysis of the institutions through which that system is transmitted and enforced' (1970, p. 21).

[29] Kuhn 1962.

[30] Mead 1974.

[31] Skinner 1977, p. 1.

[32] Skinner 1972, pp. 12-25.

[33] Saussure 1959, p. 11-12 (original emphasis). This description is a bit simplistic compared with current understandings, but the principle that the association of sound-images with concepts is made by each individual is still valid.

[34] Glasersfeld 1995, p. 134.

[35] Vygotsky 1962, p. 151.

[36] Karl Popper, for example, acknowledged that, 'The old scientific ideal of *episteme*—of absolutely certain, demonstrable knowledge—has proved to be an idol. The demand for scientific objectivity makes it inevitable that every scientific statement must remain tentative forever. It may indeed be corroborated, but every corroboration is relative to other statements which, again, are tentative' (1959, p. 280).

[37] Belton 2002.

[38] For example: Smith & The Drawing Study Group 1998; Wilson & Wilson 1982. I recall a personal experience of art education in my first year of high school. Assessment was based on the 'quality' of art works produced and on a test of art knowledge. I scored 100% for the test, but only 53% for the course overall.

[39] Belton 2002, p. 8.

[40] Albert Einstein, for example, saw that 'Pure logical thinking cannot yield us any knowledge of the empirical world; all knowledge of reality starts from experience and ends in it. Propositions arrived at by purely logical means are completely empty as regards reality' (1954, p. 271).

[41] Michael Crotty observes, also, that 'These viewpoints—seeing interpretation as essentially an identification of authorial intent, or looking instead to an intention intrinsic to the text as such, or making the reader pivotal in the generation of meaning—are embodied, with their many variants, in the history of both literary criticism and reading comprehension theory' (1998, p. 107).

[42] In *The Psychology of Science*, Abraham Maslow describes the narrowly adaptive value of professional identities connected to the possession of particular bodies of abstract knowledge. He saw that intellectualism and science can be a defense, a way of avoiding life, and can serve a need for certainty, a need to be dominant and controlling, a need for "impressing people often at the cost of part of the truth" and a need to be "satisfied with naming rather than experiencing... (a) common shortcoming of professional intellectuals" (1966, pp. 26–29, 33–39).

[43] For example, in his important book, *Radical Constructivism: A Way of Knowing and Learning*, Ernst von Glasersfeld (1995) draws upon many thinkers and researchers, including Piaget, in support of an extended argument for a more profound version of constructivism. He refers to this version as 'radical', in order to emphasise that it involves a

complete revision of traditional epistemology's concepts of knowledge, truth, understanding and communication. Glasersfeld observed that the many authors who began professing a constructivist orientation in the 1970s in response to Jean Piaget's work, focused on the relatively trivial notion that individuals build up cognitive structures. My own experience in many and varied education contexts confirms that, where teachers and other educators are aware at all of the notion of constructivism, they tend to see it as suggesting that knowledge is built up ("so let's first find out what students already know"), rather than as having any implications for the nature of knowledge and knowing itself, or for the nature of the world we engage with. A fuller sense of constructivism recognises that our knowledge is an interpretation and the world we engage with is dynamic. Today is never yesterday. 'So what remains is, again, the constructivist hypothesis,' concluded Piaget, for example, 'and is it not quite plausible to think of the nature that underlies physical reality as constantly in process of construction rather than as a heap of finished structures? (1971b, p. 68)'

[44] Innumerable researchers have drawn this conclusion. They include Bloom 1964; Dewey 1931, 1938; Freire 1972a, 1976; Glasersfeld 1995; Goleman 1996; Heidegger 1996; James 1983; Koestler 1969; Marx 1963, 1996; Merleau-Ponty 1962; Ortega y Gasset 1946, 1958; Pert 1997; 2000; Piaget 1955, 1970, 1971a, 1973, 1974; Powers 1973, 1998; Sternberg 1985, 1988; Young & Klosko 1994; Young, Klosko & Weishaar 2006. This understanding is also reflected in a 1999 summary of implications for education of brain research (ASCD 1999).

[45] See, for example, ASCD 1999; Dewey 1931, pp. 235, 242; Freire 1972a, p. 64; 1972b, p. 31; Glasersfeld 1995; Goleman 1996, p. 176; Marx 1963, p. 159; 1996, p. 121; Pert 1997; 2000; Piaget 1955, p. 311; 1970, p. 15; 1971a, p. 10; 1973, p. 38; and Powers 1973; 1998.

[46] Powers 1973, 1979, 1989, 1990, 1998.

[47] Pert 1997; 2000.

[48] Pert 2000, Disc 1, Part 2.

[49] Pert 2000, Disc 3, Part 6.

[50] Merton 1968, p. 475.

[51] Merton 1968, p. 476.

[52] Rosenthal & Lawson 1964.

[53] Rosenthal & Jacobson 1968.

[54] This study became famous in education circles. Unfortunately, my

observation has been that teachers generally miss the point. They tend not to recognise the significance of the insight that *implicitly* held beliefs, attitudes and intentions of human beings are *subtly* creative. Rather, they have tended to conclude that if they consciously expect more from students, or in other words 'demand more', they'll get more, and this often translates as just putting more performance pressure on students.

[55] Goswami 1995, p. 42.

[56] Goswami 1995, p. 43.

[57] Goswami 1995.

[58] Emoto 2004, p. xxiv.

[59] Emoto 2004, p. xxv.

[60] Pert 2000, Disc 1, Part 11.

[61] Cited in Pert 1997, p. 147.

[62] Lipton 2005, p. 139.

[63] Lipton 2005, pp. 140-41.

[64] Pert 1997, p. 289; Pert 2000, Disc 3, Part 3.

[65] Geertz 1993, p. 44.

[66] Wilde 1895.

[67] Gadamer 1995, p. 276.

[68] José Ortega y Gasset describes such meanings 'received from without' (1958, p. 101) as 'masks of thinking', 'trappings' and 'screens' (1946, pp. 59-63), 'decrepit and devoid of evidence' (1958, p. 101). He observes that instead of engaging experientially with the world, we find ourselves 'living on top of a culture which has already become false' (1958, p. 100). For Martin Heidegger, the 'public way in which things have been interpreted' is a seduction and a domination, in which 'the they unfolds its true dictatorship... [and] determines what and how one "sees"' (1996, pp. 119, 159). And Karl Marx observed that, through our immersion in abstractions, the world of nature and objects comes to be seen as external, alien and hostile, and, ultimately, to include 'alien and hostile men' (1963, p. 200; 1976, p. 177).

[69] Arthur Koestler, for example, conceding that to some extent the behaviourist view of the human being as a conditioned automaton is valid, observes that, 'When the same task is encountered under relatively unchanging conditions in a monotonous environment, the responses will become stereotyped, flexible skills will degenerate into rigid patterns, and the person will more and more resemble an automaton, governed by fixed habits, whose actions and ideas move in narrow grooves' (1969, pp. 118-119).

[70] John Dewey observed that, 'A true aim is thus opposed at every point to an aim which is imposed upon a process of action from without. The latter is fixed and rigid; it is not a stimulus to intelligence in the given situation, but is an externally dictated order to do such and such things... In education, the currency of these externally imposed aims is responsible for the emphasis put upon the notion of preparation for a remote future and for rendering the work of both teacher and pupil mechanical and slavish' (1916, p. 129).

[71] The term 'counter-control' refers to the phenomenon that people act to oppose and cancel the effects of things in the world that might disturb the perceptions they are controlling for, and make them change (Ford & Bourbon n.d.). Perceptual Control Theory makes clear that efforts to control the behaviour (including the learning) of another person through force or coercion are ultimately counter-productive. Even the arch behaviourist, B.F. Skinner, acknowledged that when you seek to control other people, you have to be prepared to be counter-controlled by them (1953, p. 321).

[72] See, for example, Goldberg 1983, pp. 217-219.

[73] John Holt, for example, contrasts 'the affected, guarded, held-in, furtive, timid, sneaky, and sullen or seductive children I see [in most schools, with] the unaffected, natural, bold, vital, frank, open, and honest children' he observed during several visits to a school where there were no outcome evaluations, grades or reports (2004, p. 121).

[74] Pert 1997, pp. 142-43.

[75] Jean Piaget referred to this kind of learning, where a new operating pattern (action scheme) is formed, as 'accommodation' (1974, pp. 335-336).

[76] A similar process of operating pattern reconstruction is described by, for example, Dewey 1931, Freire 1976, Glasersfeld 1995, Koestler 1969, Piaget 1974, Powers 1973, 1998, and Sternberg 1988.

[77] Sinclair 1994, p. 109. This is also, of course, a very succinct way of explaining one of the core reasons why the vast amount of insights and evidence I have pulled together in this book (and much that I haven't mentioned) regarding the inadequacy or invalidity of the currently dominant assumptions and practices of school education is seldom, if ever, given any attention.

[78] Arthur Koestler, for example, identifies the point at which the view of human beings as conditioned automatons ceases to be viable, as the creative act of 'bisociation'. Habit is defeated by originality in an 'act of liberation' (1969, p. 96), when the creative act makes

connections between previously isolated conditioned operating patterns. 'The bisociative act connects previously unconnected matrices of experience; it makes us "understand what it is to be awake, to be living on several planes at once"' (1969, p. 45). Critical thinking and self-analysis will not effectively release us from our conditioned operating patterns.

[79] Bastick 1982, p. 2.

[80] Koestler 1969, p. 146.

[81] Tolle 2004, p. 24. As Arthur Koestler observed, 'The rules of the game, however absurd, cannot be altered by playing that game. Among all forms of mentation, verbal thinking is the most articulate, the most complex, and the most vulnerable to infectious diseases. It is liable to absorb whispered suggestions, and to incorporate them as hidden persuaders into the code. Language can become a screen which stands between the thinker and reality. This is the reason why true creativity often starts where language ends' (1969, p. 177).

[82] Belton 2002, pp. 8-15.

[83] Belton (2002, p. 12) uses the terms 'meanings' and 'significances' to distinguish between intended and interpreted meanings, respectively, in a way parallel to Eric Hirsch's (1967, pp. 142-143) use of those terms to draw a distinction between hermeneutics and literary criticism, respectively.

[84] Belton 2002, p. 12.

[85] Taylor 2008a.

[86] Taylor 2008b, pp. 69-70.

[87] Tolle 2004, pp. 3-6.

[88] Fukuoka 1978, pp. 8-10.

[89] Tolle 2004, p. 13.

[90] Fukuoka 1985, p. 120.

[91] Tolle 2004, pp. 23-24.

[92] Fromm 1974, pp. 26-31.

[93] Quoted in Buhner 2004, p. 155.

[94] Quoted in Hart 2003, p. 42. "Ellen" is a research pseudonym.

[95] Quoted in Buhner 2004, pp. 176, 178.

[96] Alfassa 1992, p. xvii.

[97] Quoted in Buhner 2004, p. 155.

[98] Pert 1997, p. 146; Taylor 2008a.

[99] Taylor 2008a.

[100] Hart 2003, pp. 9-10.

[101] For example, Hart and a colleague conducted a sophisticated,

statistical, anonymous survey of 450 young adults, asking about specific kinds of spiritual experiences. The number who indicated they had had particular experiences ranged from 10% to more than 80%. Of those who indicated an age at which they first had these experiences, between 60% and 90% indicated that it was during childhood. (2003, p. 6.)

[102] Hart 2003, pp. 4, 14.

[103] For eloquent articulations of this insight see, for example, James 1910 and Emerson 1987.

APPENDIX A

GENRE GUIDES

⚛

THE SCIENTIFIC EXPERIMENT GENRE

Purpose
The scientific method seeks to generate interpretations of the workings of the world that are reliable, because they have been tested in particular ways which have provided evidence.

Structure
The basic structure of scientific inquiry consists of nine steps.

Ask a Question: We identify, or become aware of, an issue or question we wish to have more reliable knowledge of. For example, "Why does A happen to B?"

Formulate a Hypothesis: In answer to the question, we make a tentative statement, called a hypothesis, which we will test. For example, "C alone causes A to happen to B".

Select a Sample: We select a sample, or small portion of all the things to which our hypothesis might apply. That is, we select a sample of all the Bs which exist.

Create a Control Group: We use part of the sample as a control group, which won't be experimented on.

Design the Experiment: As we design an experiment to test the hypothesis, we try to control possible errors by removing as many as possible of the factors, called variables, that could interfere with the subject of the experiment. That is, we remove other variables which could cause A to happen to B.

Conduct the Experiment: Under these controlled conditions, we conduct the actual experiment. That is, in the experimental group, we subject B to the influence of C. In the control group, all conditions are identical to the experimental group, except that we do not subject B to the influence of C.

Observe and Record Changes: We observe and record any changes where

A happens to B, noting the degree of changes and the number of items in each group which show a change.

Analyse the Findings: We carefully consider the results.

Write a Report: We write a report of the experiment, which includes a description of methods, findings and conclusions.

Language Features and Conventions

Issues for investigation are generally expressed as questions. Hypotheses are expressed as statements. Words associated with cause and effect are commonly used, such as "when..., then...", "why does", "results in", "causes", "changes from... to...", "happens when". Informal lists may be used to identify required apparatus (experimental equipment and materials). Date and time are usually recorded as the experiment and observations progress. Records of observations may include the use of tables and tally marks, diagrams and/or brief complete sentences.

Short Example

Ask a Question: Why do plants grown indoors sometimes wilt and die, even though they get plenty of water?

Formulate a Hypothesis: Lack of light causes plants to wilt and die.

Select a Sample: We will use six, two-week old tomato seedlings. All six plants are from the same source, are in the same size pots, and are growing in the same kind of potting mix.

Create a Control Group: Three plants will be placed near a well-lit window, but out of direct sunlight.

Design the Experiment: Three plants will be placed in a cupboard near the centre of the same room, so that little or no natural or artificial light reaches them. The cupboard door will be left ajar, so that room temperature air can freely circulate around the plants. The control group and experimental group plants will be watered the same amount, at the same times each day. No other special treatments will be applied to one group at the exclusion of the other.

Conduct the Experiment: All items and environmental conditions are set up.

Observe and Record Changes: Once each day for eight days, observations of the condition of each of the plants is made and recorded.

Plant	Day 1	Day 2	Day 3	Day 4	Day 5	Day 6	Day 7	Day 8
Cont.1	Green Strong 5mm	Green Strong 5mm	Green Strong 6mm	Green Strong 6mm	Green Strong 5mm	Green Strong 6mm	Green Strong 5mm	Green Strong 5mm
Cont.2	Green Strong 5mm	Green Strong 5mm	Green Strong 6mm	Green Strong 7mm	Green Strong 5mm	Green Strong 7mm	Green Strong 5mm	Green Strong 5mm
Cont.3	Green Strong 4mm	Green Strong 5mm	Green Strong 6mm	Green Strong 6mm	Green Strong 5mm	Green Strong 6mm	Green Strong 5mm	Green Strong 4mm
Exp.1	Green Strong 5mm	Green Weak 3mm	Green Weak 4mm	Pale Weak 2mm	Pale Weak 2mm	Pale Limp 1mm	V.Pale Limp 0mm	Dead
Exp.2	Green Strong 5mm	Green Weak 3mm	Green Weak 3mm	Pale Weak 2mm	Pale Weak 2mm	Pale Weak 2mm	V.Pale Limp 1mm	V.Pale Limp 0mm
Exp.3	Green Strong 6mm	Green Weak 3mm	Green Weak 3mm	Pale Weak 2mm	Pale Weak 2mm	Pale Weak 1mm	V.Pale Limp 1mm	V.Pale Limp 0mm

Analyse the Findings: All three (100%) of the control group plants remained in a healthy state over the eight-day experimental period. Their average growth total was 43mm, and their average daily growth was 5.3mm. The health of all three experimental plants deteriorated over the eight-day experimental period. One of the experimental plants (33%) was dead at the end of eight days, while two (67%) were very pale and limp. The average growth total for the experimental group was 17.7mm, while their average daily growth was 2.2mm, only 41.5% of the daily growth rate of the control group.

Write a Report: See the investigation report genre for how to write a report.

THE SURVEY/QUESTIONNAIRE GENRE

Purpose

The purpose of surveys and questionnaires is to collect information on the views and/or circumstances of other people. The survey seeks to gather data from a larger number of people, on a smaller number of issues or questions, and therefore lends itself to statistical analysis. The questionnaire seeks to gather data from a more limited number of people, but of a more in-depth nature, or on a wider variety of issues or questions. It may be analysed statistically too, but lends itself more to analysis and representation through description and discussion.

Structure

The structure of surveys and questionnaires is similar, but surveys have fewer questions, and usually invite shorter responses, such as ticks, a continuum and yes/no responses, whereas questionnaires have more questions and seek more in-depth responses. They may invite tick, yes/no and continuum responses, but often seek comments as well. Survey questions are often asked of people verbally, and they may not involve presenting people with printed material (though the investigator will generally have a written series of questions, and physically record responses), whereas a questionnaire is generally filled out by the respondents themselves.

The basic structure of the survey/questionnaire genre consists of five main parts:

Title: Briefly identifies the subject of the investigation.

Instructions: Briefly explains what the respondent is asked to do. Surveys generally do not ask the name of the respondents; questionnaires may or may not do so.

Questions: Questions relating to the subject are organised in a logical sequence, and may be divided into sections by headings. Appropriate spaces are provided for responses, which may require ticks, marking continua, circling "Yes" or "No", circling one of a series of words, or written comments.

Acknowledgement: A brief statement of appreciation and/or instruction for submitting the survey/questionnaire.

Report: The findings of the survey/questionnaire investigation are written up in an investigation report.

Language Features and Conventions

Most language is in the form of complete questions, but may include short phrases or lists of words. Many question marks in written forms. Language has a polite, but neutral tone. There is no indication of the investigator's personal views on the questions being asked.

Short Example

(To be administered to one hundred respondents.)

DRIVING ON THE RIGHT IN AUSTRALIA

Please complete this survey by circling either "Yes" or "No" in answer to the following two questions:

Q1: Do you believe there would be fewer road accidents if everyone in the world drove on the same side of the road?	Yes	No
Q2: Since most countries currently drive on the right side of the road, would you be in favour of Australia changing to driving on the right side?	Yes	No

Thanks for helping with this survey.

THE INVESTIGATION REPORT GENRE

Purpose
The purpose of an investigation report is to present the findings of a scientific experiment or survey/questionnaire investigation, to explain the methods used to acquire them, and to discuss implications.

Structure
The basic structure of an investigation report consists of six parts:

Title: Briefly identifies the subject of the investigation.

Aim: Answers the questions, "What was investigated and why?" In a report of a scientific experiment, this usually includes a hypothesis, a tentative statement that the experiment or investigation seeks to confirm by looking for evidence which might support it or show it to be non-viable.

Method: Answers the question, "How did you go about finding out what you wanted to know?" Did you use observation, survey, questionnaire, interview, experiment? The method or methods are described in detail, including materials used.

Results: Answers the question, "What did you find?" This section just gives the data gathered, often with the aid of tables and graphs.

Discussion: Answers the question, "What does this mean?" This section gives some discussion and explanation of the data reported in the Results section.

Conclusions: This final section answers the question, "So what?" It discusses the significance of what was found. It considers whether anything should be done about what was found?

An investigation report may also include a reference list, when appropriate.

Language Features and Conventions

The investigation report is given a title, which identifies the specific subject of the investigation. The report focuses on establishing what was observed or discovered, not on feelings or opinions, though these may play some part in the final section. Therefore, there is generally no use of personal words, such as "I did this", "we did that", "you can tell". The investigation report uses formal language, consisting always of sentences, except the list of any materials used. Most parts of the report should be written in the past tense and, particularly in a scientific report, should be clear and exact. For example, it would not be appropriate to write, "The stuff was added to a glass thing with water in it". Rather, "10ml of hydrochloric acid were added to a glass beaker containing 100ml of water". Bulky material, such as survey forms or tally sheets, are attached as an appendix at the back of the report. Various methods of summary are used to present findings, in particular tables and graphs.

Short Example

DRIVING ON THE RIGHT IN AUSTRALIA

Aim

The people of Australia have become increasingly concerned about the number of road accidents, particularly fatalities, resulting from confusion about positioning on the road. Many accidents occur when drivers who are used to driving on the right-hand side of the road in other countries, become confused and disoriented when driving on the left in Australia.

Many measures have been used by police to reduce road accidents, but no serious consideration has been given to changing the road rules in Australia so that we drive on the same side of the road as people in most other countries. The purpose of this investigation was to determine the level of support for such a change among the general population.

Method

Twenty-five class members interviewed four people each, and asked them two questions, in the following order.

Do you believe there would be fewer road accidents if everyone in the world drove on the same side of the road?

Since most countries currently drive on the right side of the road, would you be in favour of Australia changing to driving on the right side?

Results

	Yes	No	Total
Q1	90	10	100
Q2	15	85	100

Discussion

A large majority (90%) of our sample of 100 people thought there would be fewer accidents if everyone in the world drove on the same side of the road, but only a small minority of the sample (15%) were in favour of Australia making a change from the left to the right side.

Conclusions

At first glance it might seem strange that most people thought it would be safer for everyone to drive on the same side, yet few people want Australia to change. However, two possible reasons seem to offer likely explanations.

The first possibility is that people do not want to pay the price of a greater number of accidents and fatalities in Australia during the change-over period. The second possibility is that people might think an idea is good in theory, but in the end, they prefer to stay with what is familiar, even though there are significant disadvantages in doing so.

Further investigation would be required to determine which of these, if either, is the explanation for the strange results of this investigation.

THE PERSUASIVE LETTER GENRE

Purpose

The purpose of a persuasive (expository) letter is to put forward, to a particular person or organisation (or, in the case of a letter to the editor, the general public), an argument or point of view on some issue of concern.

Structure

The basic structure of a persuasive letter consists of five parts:
1. Initial details, including sender's address, date, recipient's name and address, and greeting.
2. The writer's basic position or point of view is clearly stated.

3. Arguments for the point of view are presented in logical order, along with evidence, reasons and/or examples. Older children might also make some acknowledgement of the main arguments against their point of view, and answer them.
4. Summing up of argument, and restating of the point of view taken.
5. Formal sign-off.

Language Features and Conventions

The persuasive letter takes a formal tone. It is written primarily in the present tense. It makes use of full sentences and paragraphs. Paragraphs in letters are typically separated by a blank line. Linking words to do with reasoning and the idea of cause and effect are used, such as might, may, also, however, therefore, thus, so, for this reason. Common formal sign-offs include "regards" and "yours sincerely".

Short Example

11 Sample Street
MADEUPTOWN 4890
15 May 2026

Mr John Brown
Federal Minister for Transport
54 Motorcar Avenue
CANBERRA 2345

Dear Mr Brown

Most people in the world drive their cars on the right side of the road. As international travel becomes cheaper and more common, more and more people who are used to driving on the right side of the road are getting confused and causing accidents on Australian roads, where we drive on the left.

An obvious solution would be for countries in the minority, like Australia, which drive on the left side of the road, to change their rules so that all people in the world drive on the right side of the road. This would minimise confusion, and in the long term greatly reduce the number of injuries and deaths due to road accidents.

An additional benefit would be the reduction in accident repair costs and a corresponding reduction in the amount we all have to pay for car insurance.

One problem with this solution is that, for a little while there would be more confusion on Australian roads, and more accidents, while everyone got used to driving on the right side.

In the long run, though, changing to driving on the right side of the road in Australia makes sense. We should not allow some short-term disadvantages to deter us from enjoying the huge long-term advantages of making this change.

Yours sincerely

MWright
May B. Wright

THE REFERENCE LIST GENRE

Purpose
The reference list genre usually forms a part of more complex genres, such as an investigation report. The reference list provides a list of information sources that have been referred to in a work of writing. The term 'bibliography' is sometimes used to refer to a reference list, though the term 'bibliography' is more commonly used to refer to a 'stand alone' list of books, journal articles, websites and the like, on a particular subject.

Structure
The basic structure of a simple reference list consists of two parts:
Title: The title used is 'Reference List' or simply, 'References' (without the inverted commas), and does not include reference to the subject of the larger work of writing.
List of Sources: An alphabetical listing by author surname (not numbered).

Language Features and Conventions
The reference list has several distinct accepted formats. A simple format for children includes the following details in order: author surname and initial, year of publication (or of access from the Internet), title of book or article, name of journal if applicable, name of

publishing company, place of publication. Book, journal and website names are usually typed in italics. Each piece of information is separated by a comma. Special use is made of single inverted commas for journal article titles, and of square brackets for Internet URLs (Uniform Resource Locators or website addresses). For Internet URLs, the date last accessed is usually indicated in round brackets after the URL. The list of sources usually has a spare line between each source, and/or may be indented. Where a particular quotation is being referenced, or a particular page is being indicated as the source of information, the page or pages are indicated at the end of the reference as "p" for one page or "pp" for more than one page.

Short Example
References
Audi, P. 1997, 'Major causes of road accidents in Australia', *Motoring Australia*, vol. 2, no. 1, pp. 15-29.

Department of Cars 2023, *Australian Road Accident Statistics*. [http://www.doc.gov.au/transport/fictitious/statistics] (accessed 20 May 2025).

Ford, A. & Mazda, C. 1996, *Safe Driving in Australia*, Carr & Co., Brisbane.

THE LETTER OF INVITATION GENRE

Purpose
The purpose of an invitation letter is to request the attendance of a particular person, group of people, or representative of an organisation, at some particular event. The description here is of a more formal invitation, such as might be sent to a person not well known personally, rather than to a familiar friend or relative.

Structure
The basic structure of an invitation letter consists of five parts:
1. Initial details, including sender's address, date, recipient's name and address, and greeting.
2. The writer introduces him or herself and/or the organisation or group they represent.

3. The actual invitation is made, including a statement of details regarding the nature and/or purpose of the event, the time, date and place, and any special considerations regarding appropriate dress. Some indication might be given regarding others, if any, who will be attending the event. The invitation should also make clear any cost that might be involved, any items the person might be requested to bring, and any special role they might be requested to play in the event. A request for a response by a particular date should be made.

4. A brief statement indicating hopes for their attendance, or anticipation of their response, is generally made in conclusion.

5. Formal sign-off.

Language Features and Conventions

The invitation letter takes a polite, but semi-formal tone. It is not obviously persuasive, but not entirely neutral either, since there is generally a hope that the person will want to attend. It is written in a mixture of present and future tenses. It makes use of full sentences and paragraphs. Paragraphs in letters are typically separated by a blank line. Linking words and phrases to do with description and explanation are used, such as "it will be", "we hope that", "after", "during", "in order to". Common formal sign-offs include "regards" and "yours sincerely".

Short Example

62 Sample Street
MADEUPTOWN 4890
5 May 2026

Mrs Josie Burton
President
Madeuptown Chamber of Commerce
35 Business Street
MADEUPTOWN 4890

Dear Mrs Burton

My name is Harry Youngperson, and I am writing on behalf of members of the Yellow River community. We would like to invite you, or a representative of the Chamber of Commerce, to attend a special event to be held at our Community Centre at 62 Sample Street in a few weeks' time.

Some young members of our community have been working on a project to devise solutions to the difficulties many young people in our town have in finding a job when they finish their education. Our special audiovisual presentation, to commence at 11.00am on Tuesday, 27 May, will outline the findings of our investigation, and a variety of proposals we believe will help generate jobs for local young people.

During the program, several young people will receive community service awards from Mayor Jeff Beechmont. Following the proceedings, a light morning tea will be provided.

You are among a small number of local community leaders we are hoping will be able to attend the presentation. Could you please let us know if you will be able to attend, by phoning the Centre on 44556677, before Friday 23 May?

We look forward to hearing from you and seeing you at the event.

Regards

HYoungperson
Harry Youngperson
Community Centre Representative

THE LETTER OF THANKS GENRE

Purpose
An expression of appreciation may take a spoken (a "vote of thanks") or written form. Its purpose is to convey thanks to one or more people, or to an organisation, for some valued contribution, assistance or consideration. The description here is of a more formal written expression of appreciation, such as might be sent to a person not well known personally, rather than to a familiar friend or relative.

Structure
The basic structure of a written expression of appreciation consists of four parts:

1. Initial details, including sender's address, date, recipient's name and address, and greeting.
2. The actual comments of appreciation are expressed, including a statement regarding the nature, time and place of the event or situation which formed the context for the help provided. Some indication might be given of how you or others benefited from the help provided. Also, recognition should be given of the efforts, time, expense or inconvenience experienced by the person, as appropriate.
3. A brief statement of well-wishing, or possibly of further association or involvement with them in the future, is generally made in conclusion.
4. Formal sign-off, including identification of the group or organisation you represent, if appropriate.

Language Features and Conventions
The written expression of appreciation takes a polite, semi-formal tone. It is written in a mixture of present and past tenses. It makes use of full sentences and paragraphs. Paragraphs in letters are typically separated by a blank line. Linking words and phrases to do with description, benefits and thanks are used, such as "it was good to", "we learned a lot", "we appreciated", "thanks again". Common formal sign-offs include "regards" and "yours sincerely". In the case of a letter of thanks, the tone would usually be a bit less formal, so "regards" or the warmer "kind regards" would be appropriate sign-offs.

Short Example
Yellow River Community Centre
11 Sample Street
MADEUPTOWN 4890
3 June 2026

Mrs Josie Burton
President
Yellow River Chamber of Commerce
35 Business Street
YELLOW RIVER 4100

Dear Mrs Burton

I am writing on behalf of the members of the Yellow River community to thank you for attending the presentation at our Community Centre last Tuesday. We realise the many commitments and busy schedule you have in your work, and do appreciate your willingness to find time to attend the event.

In particular, we appreciated the special interest you showed in the efforts of some community members to devise solutions to the difficulties many young people in our town have in finding a job when they finish school. It was great to hear you make a commitment on behalf of the Chamber of Commerce to further investigate the viability of some of the proposals made. Several members of the community have commented how glad they feel that their hard work promises to have some real benefit in the local community.

We look forward to further communication and association with you and the Chamber of Commerce in the future.

Kind regards

HYoungperson
Harry Youngperson
Community Centre Representative

THE RECOUNT GENRE

Purpose
The purpose of a recount is to list and describe past experiences by retelling events in the order in which they happened (chronological order).

Structure
The basic structure of a recount consists of three parts:
1. The setting or orientation—background information answering who, when, where and why?
2. Events are identified and described in chronological order.
3. Concluding comments express a personal opinion regarding the events described.

Language Features and Conventions
The recount has a title, which summarises the subject of the text. Past

tense verbs are used, and frequent use is made of words which link events in time, such as next, later, when, then, after, before, first. Recounts describe events, so plenty of use is made of verbs (action words), and of adverbs (which describe or add more detail to verbs).

Short Example
MY DAY AT THE BEACH

Last week my friend and I were bored after three weeks of holidays, so we rode our bikes to Long Beach, which is only five kilometres from where I live. When we arrived at the beach, we were surprised to see there was hardly anyone there.

After having a quick dip in the ocean, which was really cold, we realised one reason there were not many people there. It was also quite windy.

After we bought ourselves some hot chips at the takeaway store nearby, we rode our bikes down the beach for a while, on the hard, damp part of the sand. We had the wind behind us and, before we knew it, we were several kilometres down the beach.

Before we made the long trip back we decided to paddle our feet in the water for a while, and then sit down for a rest. While we were sitting on the beach, just chatting, it suddenly dawned on us both that all the way back we would be riding into the strong wind!

When we finally made it back home, we were both totally exhausted!

But we learned some good lessons that day!

REAL-WORLD INVESTIGATION
PLANNING PROFORMA AND EXAMPLE

❦

HOW CAN WE PROMOTE SUSTAINABLE ENERGY?
An Investigation of Our Technological World for Around Age 12
(This transdisciplinary approach to curriculum integration dissolves boundaries between the disciplines and addresses issues of relevance, interest and construction of meaning through exploring real-world issues, questions and objectives.)

Curriculum Aims or Objectives Addressed in the Investigation
Mandated objectives from a variety of subject, discipline or learning areas could be identified here.

Real-world Contexts, Needs or Purposes Driving the Investigation
Fossil fuels provide over 80% of the world's energy. These fuels, most importantly coal, oil and gas, will not last forever—they are non-renewable resources. They are also damaging to the environment in a variety of ways. There is, therefore, an increasing need to develop and promote new forms of energy.

Generic Curriculum Elements that May Support the Investigation
Design, make, evaluate (scale model, following production procedures, and gathering and responding to feedback when designing and applying production systems)
Email
Explanation – written
Explanatory diagram / Design plan Graph
Information literacy (sourcing, evaluating and using the practical advice of others)
Letter of invitation

Letter of persuasion (exposition)
Oral/Multimedia presentation (including Information and Communication Technologies)
Promotional flier/leaflet Promotional poster Scale model
Scientific experiment
Scientific experiment report
Social investigation report
Summary/Précis
Survey/Questionnaire
Table
Webpage making
Word processing

Understandings Essential to the Investigation

Basic concepts and principles relating to forces and motion.
Basic concepts and principles relating to energy, including its forms, sources, uses, conversion and conservation.
Systems and sub-systems assist in translating design ideas into products which meet particular needs.
Other mandated curriculum content seen to be relevant to the investigation.

Methods of Assessing Understandings and Generic Curriculum Elements

A variety of mandated assessment instruments and methods can be used to assess the child's understanding of the mandated knowledge content and their use of genres, either during or at the conclusion of the investigation. Parent observations of the child's performance, parent-child discussions at different stages of the project, and student self-reflection and self-ratings may also be appropriate forms of evaluation.

Activities to Support Child's Experience and Effective Activity

STEP 1 ~ NEGOTIATE ISSUE
(If this investigation is undertaken in order to address mandated curriculum objectives, this step will generally not apply.)

STEP 2 ~ CLARIFY EXPECTATIONS
(Externally mandated assessment requirements, unlike those in a purely child-initiated investigation, can be explained to the child as the

investigation unfolds, and might only be flagged in very general terms at the commencement of the investigation.)

STEP 3 ~ ORIENTATION

Consider artistic/photographic interpretations of the energy crisis, and create an artistic interpretation.

Decorate room and/or make collage with magazine pictures showing benefits of energy.

Consider poetic and song lyric perspectives (e.g. Julian Lennon, *Salt Water Runs in My Eyes*).

Read some fiction or non-fiction about climate change, Greenhouse Effect, or energy crisis.

Think and discuss. What is energy? Where does it come from? What good effects does it have? What bad effects?

Consider various statistics regarding the energy crisis.

Create a crossword puzzle with words and clues relating to this topic. Invite a grandparent or family friend to do the puzzle.

Define the problem / identify what's 'known' and what needs to be 'known'. 5W+H (who, what, when, where, why, how). What do you know already?

Asking 5W+H in relation to the past, the present, what could be done, what is likely to be done, what do various people intend to do?

STEP 4 ~ INFORMATION GATHERING

Options: Surveys, questionnaires, interviews, writing/faxing to request information, emailing, telephoning, Internet search, experiment, trial, observation, excursion (petrol company? solar powered facility or house? solar company or solar powered facility?), online/print encyclopaedia, YouTube, fiction and non-fiction texts, find and follow a WebQuest on sustainable energy (try www.webquest.org).

Survey family members and family friends regarding energy concerns/actions.

A home energy audit? Develop a rating scale for domestic or organisation energy practices.

Science experiment.

Recent newspaper articles on energy crisis or alternative energy.

STEP 5 ~ INFORMATION PROCESSING (DESIGN)

Processing of information gathered e.g. creating tables and graphs from survey (possibility: Create a graph online or in MS Excel).

Assumption testing. How have others seen the problem? Who benefits

from the continued use of non-renewable energy?
Include a kinaesthetic science experiment such as bicycle (environmentally friendly) stopping distances (with science report, chart, graph, statistical analysis?).
Reading and questioning texts (including songs? poems?). Think and discuss. Who benefits? Who suffers? Who has suggested alternatives?

STEP 6 ~ APPLICATION
Make, apply, propose, promote.
(The following items are obviously designed then made, planned then written and sent, etcetera.)
Persuasive letter (to local, state or federal politician? business? other groups?)
Newsletter item.
Radio advertisement for solar or solar/petrol car.
Petition.
Make a poster promoting renewable energy.
Other responses?

STEP 7 ~ EVALUATION
Reflection, testing, consultation regarding suitability of solutions, proposals or responses.
PMI (Plus, Minus, Interesting) or SWOT (Strengths, Weaknesses, Opportunities, Threats) analysis based on: Did we influence anybody? Or will we? How did you feel about the investigation? Did you benefit from the investigation? How? How might you do things differently in future?
Self-assessment.
Parent evaluation

STEP 8 ~ PRESENTATION
Who to? Why?
Consider including in the presentation, if one is made:
Graphs?
A personally composed poem?
A personally drawn cartoon?
A rap song?
A musical (recorded) collage?
A personally created board game?
A drawn diagram (scanned?) of an alternative energy source and/or a model/diorama to scale?

STEP 9 ~ ASSESSMENT

See information in the above section headed "Methods of Assessing Understandings and Generic Curriculum Elements". Most assessment will not be chronologically the last step in the investigation.

Resources to Support the Investigation

Web searches on sustainable energy and clean energy will find many resources that might be useful. Searches can also be done on such topics as force, laws of motion, types of energy, and the search for new sources of energy. Of course, the local library will also have resources.

OTHER POSSIBLE REAL-WORLD INVESTIGATION TOPICS

The above is an example of a real-world investigation outline that could assist parents in satisfying some of the curriculum and assessment requirements that education authorities may be imposing on home-schoolers. Here are some other topics that could be adapted to that purpose in a somewhat similar way.

How Can We Make Places Healthy and Safe?
What Can Families Be Like?
Using the World Around Us to Make Things
Can We Use Paper Without Damaging the Earth?
What Kind of Me Would I Like to Be?
Why Do Different Groups Do Things Differently?
Making Toys and Games from the World Around Us
How Does My Garden Grow?
How Do Animals and People Stay Healthy?
What Makes a Good Place to Live?
Keeping Warm, Keeping Cool
Can We Minimise Environmental Disasters?
Taking Action on Hunger and Malnutrition
Planning an Event to Celebrate Difference
Changing Materials to Make ... Dinner!
How Can We Enjoy and Care for Nature?
How Can We Deal with Hazards and Emergencies?
How Do People Co-operate in Societies?
How Can We Build a More Useful Landscape?
What's it Like in Your Part of the World?

How Can We Promote a Healthy Lifestyle?
How Can We Get Along in the Global Village?
How Do I Go About Building a Structure?
How Can We Stop Damaging Ecosystems?
How Can We Deal with Risk in Social Environments?
Can We Learn from the Past and Create the Future?

REFERENCES

Abramowitz, Stephen, Gormes, Beverly, & Abramowitz, Christine 1975, 'Publish or politic: Referee bias in manuscript review', *Journal of Applied Social Psychology*, vol. 5, no. 3, pp. 187-200.

Alfassa, Mirra (The Mother) 1992, *Flowers and Their Hidden Messages*, Sri Aurobindo Ashram Publications, Pondicherry. First published 1973.

Arkes, Hal & Harkness, Allan 1983, 'Estimates of contingency between two dichotomous variables', *Journal of Experimental Psychology: General*, vol. 112, no. 1, pp. 117-135.

ASCD 1999, *The Human Brain: An ASCD Professional Enquiry Kit*, Association for Supervision and Curriculum Development, Alexandria, VA. (Kit).

Atkin, Julia 1999, *Reconceptualising the Curriculum for the Knowledge Era: Part 1 – The Challenge*, Seminar Series No. 81, IARTV, Melbourne, VIC.

Ball, Deborah & Cohen, David 1999, 'Developing practice, developing practitioners: Towards a practice-based theory of professional education', in Linda Darling-Hammond & Gary Sykes (eds.), *Teaching as the Learning Profession: Handbook of Policy and Practice*, Jossey-Bass, San Francisco, CA, pp. 3-31.

Barber, Bernard 1961, 'Resistance by scientists to scientific discovery', *Science*, vol. 134, no. 3479, pp. 596-602.

Barratt, Robyn 1999, 'Middle schooling: A challenge for policy and curriculum', *Education Horizons*, vol. 5, no. 3, pp. 6-9.

Bastick, Tony 1982, *Intuition: How We Think and Act*, John Wiley & Sons, Chichester.

Belton, Robert 2002, 'Introduction', in Robert Belton (ed.), *Art: The World of Art, from Aboriginal to American Pop, Renaissance to Postmodernism*, Five Mile Press, Rowville, VIC., pp. 8-15.

Black Elk 1988, *The Sacred Pipe: Black Elk's Account of the Seven Rites of the Oglala Sioux*, rec. & ed. Joseph Epes Brown, University of Oklahoma Press, Norman, OK. Photo reprint of 1953 edn.

Black, Paul & Atkin, J. Myron (eds.) 1996, *Changing the Subject:*

Innovations in Science, Mathematics and Technology Education, Routledge, London.

Buhner, Stephen 2004, *The Secret Teachings of Plants: The Intelligence of the Heart in the Direct Perception of Nature*, Bear & Company, Rochester, NY.

Cairney, Trevor 1987, 'The social foundations of literacy, *Australian Journal of Reading*, vol. 10, no. 2, pp. 84-96.

Cairney, Trevor 1988, 'Teaching reading comprehension: The development of critical and creative readers', *Australian Journal of Reading*, vol. 11, no. 3, pp. 184-194.

Cano-Garcia, Francisco & Hughes, Elaine 2000, 'Learning and thinking styles: An analysis of their interrelationship and influence on academic achievement', *Educational Psychology*, vol. 20, no. 4, pp. 413-427.

Carrington, Victoria 2002, *The Middle Years of Schooling in Queensland: A Way Forward*, Position paper prepared for Education Queensland, Brisbane, QLD.

Corey, Gerald 1996, *Theory and Practice of Counseling and Psychotherapy*, Brooks/Cole Publishing, Pacific Grove, CA.

Cornell, Joseph 1989, *Sharing Nature With Children II*, Dawn Publications, Nevada City, CA.

Cornell, Joseph 1998, *Sharing Nature With Children: The Classic Parents' and Teachers' Nature Awareness Guidebook*, Second Edition, Dawn Publications, Nevada City, CA.

Clarke, Desmond 2006, *Descartes: A Biography*, Cambridge University Press, Cambridge.

Crocker, Jennifer 1981, 'Judgement of covariation by social perceivers', *Psychological Bulletin*, vol. 90, no. 2, pp. 272-292.

Crotty, Michael 1998, *The Foundations of Social Research: Meaning and Perspective in the Research Process*, Allen & Unwin, Crows Nest, NSW.

Cuban, Larry 1984, *How Teachers Taught: Constancy and Change in American Classrooms, 1890-1980*, Longman, New York, NY.

Deal, Terrence 1990, 'Reframing reform', *Educational Leadership*, vol. 47, no. 8, May, pp. 6-12.

Descartes, René 1641, 'Second meditation', in René Descartes, *Meditations on First Philosophy*, trans. John Cottingham 1996, Cambridge University Press.

Dewey, John 1916, *Education and Democracy: An Introduction to the Philosophy of Education*, MacMillan, New York, NY.

Dewey, John 1931, *Philosophy and Civilization*, Putnam's Sons, New York, NY.

Dewey, John 1938, *Logic: The Theory of Inquiry*, Henry Holt, New York, NY.

Einstein, Albert 1954, *Ideas and Opinions*, trans. Sonja Bargmann, Crown, New York, NY.

Eisner, Elliot 1991, *The Enlightened Eye: Qualitative Inquiry and the Enhancement of Educational Practice*, Macmillan, New York, NY.

Emerson, Ralph Waldo 1987, 'Heroism', in Alfred Ferguson & Jean Ferguson Carr (eds.), *The Essays of Ralph Waldo Emerson*, Belknap Press of Harvard University Press, Cambridge, MA, pp. 143-156. First published 1841.

Emoto, Masaru 2004, *The Hidden Messages in Water*, trans. David Thayne, Beyond Words Publishing, Hillsboro, OR.

Erikson, Erik 1965, *Childhood and Society*, Penguin, Harmondsworth.

Field, Evelyn 2007, *Bully Blocking: Six Secrets to Help Children Deal with Teasing and Bullying*, Finch, Lane Cove, NSW.

Foerster, Heinz von 1981, *Observing Systems*, Intersystems Publications, Seaside, CA.

Ford, Ed 1994, *Discipline for Home and School: Book One*, Third Edition, Brandt Publishing, Scottsdale, AZ.

Ford, Ed & Bourbon, Tom n.d., *The Heart of the Process*, Brandt Publishing, Scottsdale, AZ. (video).

Freire, Paolo 1972a, *Pedagogy of the Oppressed*, trans. Myra Ramos, Penguin Education, Harmondsworth.

Freire, Paolo 1972b, *Cultural Action for Freedom*, Penguin Education, Harmondsworth. First published 1970.

Freire, Paolo 1976, *Education: The Practice of Freedom*, Writers and Readers Publishing Cooperative, London. First published 1974.

Fromm, Erich 1949, *Man for Himself: An Inquiry into the Psychology of Ethics*, Routledge & Kegan Paul, London.

Fromm, Erich 1974, *The Art of Loving*, Perennial Library, New York, NY.

Fromm, E. 1976, *To Have or To Be?* Harper & Row, New York, NY.

Fukuoka, Masanobu 1978, *The One Straw Revolution: An Introduction to Natural Farming*, trans. Chris Pearce, Tsune Kurosawa & Larry Korn, Rodale Press, Emmaus, PA.

Fukuoka, Masanobu 1985, *The Natural Way of Farming: The Theory and Practice of Green Philosophy*, Japan Publications, Tokyo.

Fullan, Michael 2001, *The New Meaning of Educational Change*, Teachers College Press, New York, NY.

Gadamer, Hans-Georg 1995, *Truth and Method*, trans. Joel Weinsheimer & Donald Marshall, Continuum, New York, NY.

First published 1960.

Geertz, Clifford 1993, *The Interpretation of Cultures: Selected Essays*, Fontana, London. First published 1973.

Gerstner, Louis, Semerad, Roger, Doyle, Denis, & Johnston, William 1994, *Reinventing Education: America's Public Schools*, Dutton, New York, NY.

Glasersfeld, Ernst von 1995, *Radical Constructivism: A Way of Knowing and Learning*, RoutledgeFalmer, London.

Glatthorn, Allan & Jailall, Jerry 2000, 'Curriculum for the new millennium', in Ronald Brandt (ed.), *Education in a New Era*, Association for Supervision and Curriculum Development, Alexandria, VA., pp. 97-121.

Goldberg, Philip 1983, *The Intuitive Edge: Understanding Intuition and Applying It in Everyday Life*, Jeremy P. Tarcher, Los Angeles, CA.

Goleman, Daniel 1996, *Emotional Intelligence: Why It Can Matter More Than IQ*, Bloomsbury, London.

Goodlad, John, Klein, M. Frances, & Associates 1974, *Looking Behind the Classroom Door: A Useful Guide to Observing Schools in Action*, Charles A. Jones, Worthington, OH.

Goodstein, Leonard & Brazis, Karen 1970, 'Credibility of psychologists, An empirical study', *Psychological Reports*, vol. 27, no. 3, pp. 835-838.

Gordon, David 1984, *The Myths of School Self-Renewal*, Teachers College Press, New York, NY.

Gorman, Michael 1986, 'How the possibility of error affects falsification on a task that models scientific problem solving', *British Journal of Psychology*, vol. 77, no. 1, pp. 85-96.

Goswami, Amit 1995, *The Self-Aware Universe: How Consciousness Creates the Material World*, Jeremy P. Tarcher/Putnam, New York, NY.

Green, Pam 1998, 'The journey from primary to secondary school: The literacy-related demands in transition', *Australian Journal of Language and Literacy*, vol. 21, no. 2, pp. 121-7.

Hanson, Norwood 1958, *Patterns of Discovery: An Inquiry into the Conceptual Foundations of Science*, Cambridge University Press, Cambridge

Hargreaves, David 1994, *The Mosaic of Learning: Schools and Teachers for the New Century*, Demos, London.

Hart, Tobin 2003, *The Secret Spiritual World of Children*, Inner Ocean, Maui.

Heidegger, Martin 1996, *Being and Time*, trans. Joan Stambaugh, State University of New York Press, Albany, NY. First published 1953.

Hirsch, Eric 1967, *Validity in Interpretation*, Yale University Press, New Haven, CT.

Hirst, Paul 1972, 'Liberal education and the nature of knowledge', in Reginald Archambault (ed.), *Philosophical Analysis and Education*, Routledge & Kegan Paul, London, pp. 113-138.

Hodas, Steven 1993, 'Technology refusal and the organisational culture of schools', *Education Policy Analysis*, vol. 1, no. 10, 14 September.

Holt, John 2004, *Instead of Education: Ways to Help People Do Things Better*, Sentient Publications, Boulder, CO. First published 1976.

Hood, David 1998, *Our Secondary Schools Don't Work Anymore*, Profile Books, Auckland.

Houts, Arthur 1989, 'Contributions of the psychology of science to metascience: A call for explorers', in Barry Gholson, William Shadish, Robert Neimeyer, & Arthur Houts (eds.), *Psychology of Science: Contributions to Metascience*, Cambridge University Press, Cambridge, pp. 47-88.

Huxley, Aldous 1962, *Island: A Novel*, Chatto & Windus, London.

Huxley, Aldous 1970, *The Perennial Philosophy*, Harper & Row, New York, N.Y. First published 1944.

James, William 1983, *Principles of Psychology*, Harvard University Press, Cambridge, MA. First published 1890.

James, William 1910, 'The Moral Equivalent of War', *McClure's Magazine*, August, pp. 463-468. Available online at [http://www.constitution.org/wj/meow.htm] (accessed 21 October 2025).

Jenkins, Herbert & Ward, William 1965, 'Judgement of contingency between responses and outcomes', *Psychological Monographs: General and Applied*, vol. 79, no. 1, pp. 1-17.

Kern, Leslie 1982, The effect of data error in inducing confirmatory inference strategies in hypothesis testing. Unpublished doctoral dissertation, Ohio State University, Kent, OH.

Klayman, Joshua & Ha, Young-Won 1987, 'Confirmation, disconfirmation, and information in hypothesis testing', *Psychological Review*, vol. 94, no. 2, pp. 211-228.

Koestler, Arthur 1969, *The Act of Creation*, Hutchinson & Co., London.

Kuhn, Thomas 1962, *The Structure of Scientific Revolutions*, University of Chicago Press, Chicago, IL.

Kuhn, Thomas 1970, 'Logic of discovery or psychology of research', in I. Lakatos & A. Musgrave (eds.), *Criticism and the Growth of*

Knowledge, Cambridge University Press, Cambridge, pp. 1-23.

Laing, R.D. 1971, *The Politics of Experience*, Penguin, Harmondsworth.

Lipton, Bruce 2005, *The Biology of Belief: Unleashing the Power of Consciousness, Matter and Miracles*, Mountain of Love/Elite Books, Santa Rosa, CA.

Lord, Charles, Ross, Lee, & Lepper, Mark 1979, 'Biased assimilation and attitude polarization: The effect of prior theories on subsequently considered evidence', *Journal of Personality and Social Psychology*, vol. 37, no. 11, pp. 2098-2109.

Loughran, John & Northfield, Jeff 1996, *Opening the Classroom Door: Teacher, Researcher, Learner*, Falmer Press, London.

Mahoney, Michael 1977, 'Publication prejudices: An experimental study of confirmatory bias in the peer review system', *Cognitive Therapy and Research*, vol. 1, no. 2, pp. 161-175.

Marr, Neil & Field, Tim 2001, *Bullycide: Death at Playtime – An Exposé of Child Suicide Caused by Bullying*, Success Unlimited, Oxfordshire.

Marx, Karl 1963, 'Economic and philosophical manuscripts', in Thomas Bottomore (ed. & trans.), *Karl Marx: Early Writings*, Watts & Co., London, pp. 61-219. Manuscripts first published 1844.

Marx, Karl 1976, *Selected Writings in Sociology and Social Philosophy*, Thomas Bottomore & Maximilien Rubel (eds.), trans. Thomas Bottomore, Penguin, Harmondsworth. First published 1956.

Marx, Karl 1996, 'Theses on Feuerbach', in Karl Marx & Frederick Engels, *The German Ideology: Part One*, Christopher Arthur (ed.), Lawrence & Wishart, London. This translation first published 1970.

Maslow, Abraham 1954, *Motivation and Personality*, Harper & Row, New York, NY.

Maslow, A. 1966, *The Psychology of Science: A Reconnaissance*, Henry Regnery Company, Chicago.

McLaren, Peter 1998, *Life in Schools: An Introduction to Critical Pedagogy in the Foundations of Education*, Longman, New York, NY.

Mead, George Herbert 1974, *Mind, Self and Society: From the Standpoint of a Social Behaviorist*, University of Chicago, Chicago, IL. First published 1934.

Merleau-Ponty, Maurice 1962, *Phenomenology of Perception*, trans. Colin Smith, Routledge & Kegan Paul, London.

Merton, Robert 1968, *Social Theory and Social Structure*, The Free Press, New York, NY. First published 1949.

Nisbett, Richard & Ross, Lee 1980, *Human Inference: Strategies and Shortcomings of Social Judgement*, Prentice-Hall, Englewood Cliffs, NJ.

Oakes, Jeannie, Quartz, Karen, Ryan, Steve, & Lipton, Martin 1999, *Becoming Good American Schools*, Jossey-Bass, San Francisco, CA.

Ortega y Gasset, Jose 1946, *Concord and Liberty*, trans. Helene Weyl, Norton, New York, NY.

Ortega y Gasset, Jose 1958, *Man and Crisis*, Norton, New York, NY.

Pert, Candice 1997, *Molecules of Emotion: The Science Behind Mind-Body Medicine*, Scribner, New York, NY.

Pert, Candice 2000, *Your Body is Your Subconscious Mind*, Sounds True, Boulder, CO. (Audio CD)

Piaget, Jean 1955, *The Construction of Reality in the Child*, trans. Margaret Cook, Routledge & Kegan Paul, London.

Piaget, Jean 1970, *Genetic Epistemology*, trans. Eleanor Duckworth, Columbia University Press, New York, NY.

Piaget, Jean 1971a, *Biology and Knowledge: An Essay on the Relations Between Organic Regulations and Cognitive Processes*, trans. Beatrix Walsh, University of Chicago Press, Chicago, IL.

Piaget, Jean 1971b, *Structuralism*, trans. Chaninah Maschler, Routledge & Kegan Paul, London. First published 1968.

Piaget, Jean 1973, *Main Trends in Inter-disciplinary Research*, Harper & Row, New York , NY.

Piaget, Jean 1974, *The Grasp of Consciousness: Action and Concept in the Young Child*, trans. Susan Wedgwood, Routledge & Kegan Paul, London.

Pinar, William 1975/2000, 'Sanity, madness, and the school', in William Pinar (ed.), *Curriculum Theorizing: The Reconceptualists*, McCutchan Publishing, Berkeley, CA, pp. 359-383.

Polanyi, Michael 1962, *Personal Knowledge: Towards a Post-Critical Philosophy*, University of Chicago Press, Chicago, IL. First published 1958.

Popper, Karl 1959, *The Logic of Scientific Discovery*, Basic Books, New York, NY. First published 1934.

Popper, Karl 1963, *Conjectures and Refutations: The Growth of Scientific Knowledge*, Routledge & Kegan Paul, London.

Powers, William 1973, *Behaviour: The Control of Perception*, Aldine, Chicago, IL.

Powers, William 1979, 'The nature of robots: Part 3. A closer look at human behavior', *Byte*, vol. 4, no. 8, July, pp. 94-116.

Powers, William 1989, *Living Control Systems: Selected Papers of William T. Powers*, Control Systems Group, Gravel Switch, KY.

Powers, William 1990, An introduction to Perceptual Control Theory: Standing at the crossroads, Paper distributed at Control Systems

Group Meeting, Indiana, Pennsylvania, August 15-19. Also available as PDF at [https://www.iapct.org/wp-content/uploads/2022/04/crossroads.pdf] (accessed 21 October 2025).

Powers, William 1998, *Making Sense of Behavior: The Meaning of Control*, Benchmark, New Canaan, CT.

Quine, Willard 1971, *From a Logical Point of View: 9 Logico-Philosophical Essays*, Harvard University Press, Cambridge, MA. First published 1953.

Ramsden, Paul 1988, 'Studying learning: Improving teaching', in Paul Ramsden (ed.), *Improving Learning: New Perspectives*, Kogan Page, London, pp. 13-31.

Rosenthal, Robert & Jacobson, Lenore 1968, *Pygmalion in the Classroom: Teacher Expectation and Pupils' Intellectual Development*, Holt, Rinehart & Winston, New York, NY.

Rosenthal, Robert & Lawson, Reed 1964, A Longitudinal Study of the Effects of Experimenter Bias on the Operant Learning of Laboratory Rats, *Journal of Psychiatric Research*, vol. 2, no. 2, pp. 61-72.

Ross, Lee & Lepper, Mark 1980, 'The perseverance of beliefs: Empirical and normative considerations', in Richard Shweder (ed.), *Fallible Judgement in Behavioral Research: New Directions for Methodology of Social and Behavioral Science*, vol. 4, Jossey-Bass, San Francisco, CA, pp. 17-36.

Ryan, James 1988, 'Conservative science in educational administration: Knowledge, power, and truth', *Journal of Educational Administration and Foundations*, vol. 3, no. 2, pp. 5-22.

Ryan, William 1976, *Blaming the Victim*, Vintage Books, New York, NY.

Sarason, Seymour 1990, *The Predictable Failure of Educational Reform: Can We Change Course Before It's Too Late?* Jossey-Bass, San Francisco, CA.

Saussure, Ferdinand de 1959, *Course on General Linguistics*, trans. Wade Baskin, Philosophical Library, New York. First published in French 1916.

Sawada, Daiyo & Caley, Michael 1985, 'Dissipative structures: New metaphors for becoming in education', *Educational Researcher*, vol. 14, no. 3, March, pp. 13-19.

Schustack, Miriam & Sternberg, Robert 1981, 'Evaluation of evidence in causal inference', *Journal of Experimental Psychology: General*, vol. 110, no. 1, pp. 101-120.

Seaton, Andrew 2020, *Spiritual Awakening Made Simple: How to See Through the Mist of the Mind to the Peace of the Here and Now*, John Hunt Publishing, Alresford.

Shaklee, Harriet & Mims, Michael 1981, 'Development of rule use in judgements of covariation between events', *Child Development*, vol. 52, no. 1, March, pp. 317-325.

Sheehan, Margaret, Marshall, Bernie, Cahill, Helen, Rowling, Louise, & Holdsworth, Roger 2000, *SchoolMatters: Mapping and Managing Mental Health in Schools*, Department of Health and Aged Care, Canberra.

Sinclair, Upton 1994, *I, Candidate for Governor: And How I Got Licked*, repr. University of California Press, Berkeley, CA. First published 1935.

Skinner, B.F. 1953, *Science and Human Behavior*, The Free Press, New York, NY.

Skinner, B.F. 1972, *Beyond Freedom and Dignity*, Jonathan Cape, London.

Skinner, B.F. 1977, 'Why I am not a cognitive psychologist', *Behaviorism*, vol. 5, no. 2, pp. 1-10.

Smith, Peter, Pepler, Debra, & Rigby, Ken 2004, *Bullying in Schools: How Successful Can Interventions Be?* Cambridge University Press, Cambridge.

Smith, Nancy, & The Drawing Study Group 1998, *Observation Drawing With Children*, Teachers College Press, New York, NY.

Snizek, William, Fuhrman, Ellsworth, & Wood, Michael 1981, 'The effect of theory group association on the evaluative content of book reviews in sociology', *American Sociologist*, vol. 16, no. 3, August, pp. 185-195.

Sternberg, Robert 1985, *Beyond IQ: A Triarchic Theory of Human Intelligence*, Cambridge University Press, Cambridge.

Sternberg, Robert 1988, *The Triarchic Mind: A New Theory of Human Intelligence*, Viking, New York, NY.

Stigler, James & Hiebert, James 1999, *The Teaching Gap: What Educators Can Learn from the World's Best Teachers*, The Free Press, New York, NY.

Stowe, John 2003, *The Findhorn Book of Connecting with Nature*, Findhorn Press, Findhorn.

Sungaila, Helen 1992, 'Educational reform and the new 'Theory of Chaos'', in Frank Crowther & Doug Ogilvie (eds.), *The New Political World of Educational Administration*, Australian Council for Educational Administration, Hawthorn, VIC., pp. 69-87.

Surprising Studies of Visual Awareness, 2003, vol. 1, Viscog Productions, Inc., Champaign, Illinois (DVD).

Taylor, Jill Bolte 2008a, 'My Stroke of Insight', [https://www.ted.com/talks/jill_bolte_taylor_my_stroke_of_insight], (accessed 21 October 2025).

Taylor, Jill Bolte 2008b, *My Stroke of Insight: A Brain Scientist's Personal Journey*, Viking, New York, NY.

Thomson, Charles & Zeuli, John 1999, 'The frame and the tapestry: Standards-based reform and professional development', in Linda Darling-Hammond & Gary Sykes (eds.), *Teaching as the Learning Profession: Handbook of Policy and Practice*, Jossey-Bass Publishers, San Francisco, CA, pp. 341-375.

Tieger, Paul & Barron-Tieger, Barbara 1997, *Nurture by Nature: Understand Your Child's Personality Type—And Become a Better Parent*, Little, Brown and Company, Boston, MA.

Tolle, Eckhart 2004, *The Power of Now: A Guide to Spiritual Enlightenment*, New World Library, Novato, CA. First published 1999.

Tuckman, Bruce 1974, 'Teaching: The application of psychological constructs', in Ronald Hyman (ed.), *Teaching: Vantage Points for Study*, Lippincott, PA.

Tzu, L. 2013, *Tao Te Ching: An Illustrated Journey* (trans. S. Mitchell), Frances Lincoln Limited, London.

Vygotsky, Lev 1962, *Thought and Language*, ed. & trans. Eugenia Haufmann & Gertrude Vakar, MIT Press, Cambridge, MA.

Ward, Jennifer 2008, *I love Dirt: 52 Activities to Help You and Your Kids Discover the Wonders of Nature*, Trumpeter, Boston, MA.

Wilde, Oscar 1895, *De Profundis*, [http://www.upword.com/wilde/de_profundis.html], (accessed 21 October 2025).

Wilson, Marjorie & Wilson, Brent 1982, *Teaching Children to Draw*, Prentice-Hall, Englewood Cliffs, NJ.

Wittgenstein, Ludwig 1969, *On Certainty*, Basil Blackwell, Oxford.

Young, Jeffrey & Klosko, Janet 1994, *Reinventing Your Life: The Breakthrough Program to End Negative Behavior... and Feel Great Again*, Plume, New York, NY.

Young, Jeffrey, Klosko, Janet, & Weishaar, Marjorie 2006, *Schema Therapy: A Practitioner's Guide*, The Guilford Press, New York, NY.

ABOUT THE AUTHOR

For more than five decades, Andrew Seaton has delved deeply into educational philosophy, psychology and methodology; old wisdom and new science; reports of higher consciousness; and a wide range of personal development, holistic wellness and spiritual awareness practices. In addition to teaching at primary, secondary and tertiary levels, he has had leadership and consultancy roles relating to school improvement and education of the 'whole person' for the 'real world'. His 2005 PhD thesis was titled, "Investing in Intelligence: An Inquiry into Educational Paradigm Change".

Andrew came to see that in our world we are generally making some deeply flawed assumptions about knowledge and human nature. In 2006, he resigned from a two-year stint in academia to live on a hobby farm, to step back from mind-based mainstream society and focus on unlearning his education and other conditioning. In the following years, he experienced major changes in his consciousness and way of being in the world. In addition to this book, he is the author of *Spiritual Awakening Made Simple: How to See Through the Mist of the Mind to the Peace of the Here and Now* (John Hunt Publishing, 2020).

Andrew is an INFJ, a lover of occasional, deep, one-on-one conversations, and a lover of solitude. But he feels that labels and concepts can no longer contain him. He feels, with Ralph Waldo Emerson, that "I am God in nature; I am a weed by the wall". He enjoys gardening, DIY, walks in a forest or on the beach, writing, singing, dancing to Creedence's "Jambalaya", and sitting in the stillness of Being. He resides on the South Coast of NSW, Australia.

Spiritual Awakening Made Simple: How to See Through the Mist of the Mind to the Peace of the Here and Now
Andrew Seaton
John Hunt Publishing, 2020

In this inspiring, and above all, practical book, Andrew Seaton guides us to our true nature as the peace-filled observing awareness beyond the mind.

The book explains how, beginning in our infancy, we experience a spiritual forgetting. The mind creates abstract interpretations of the world and who we are. These conditioned interpretations become self-fulfilling and create our life experience, our karma. Learn to see the world as it is in reality, rather than through the distorting filters of the conditioned mind. Discover how simple it is to clear away the mist of the conditioned mind and instantly drop into the awareness Self, which is who you really are.

Importantly, this book shows the reader how to avoid some of the common frustrations and traps in spiritual awakening. Perhaps best of all, it offers a simple strategy for holding in focus the ways of experiencing everyday life as the awareness Self: a simple strategy for spiritual awakening.

Spiritual Awakening Made Simple offers a concise, unified and practical formulation that will help you to awaken to your own true nature as peace, contentment and connectedness with all life.